War in the City

The bombing of Brighton and Hove

Volume II

David Rowland

Finsbury Publishing

By the same author:
War in the City, volume I
The Brighton Blitz
The Coastal Blitz
Spitfires Over Sussex: the exploits of 602 Squadron
Out of the Blue: the story of Brighton's worst air attack
Survivors: aircrew stories of World War II
On the Brighton Beat: stories about Brighton Police

Front cover: The Marine Gate flats in Brighton after the raid of 29th August, 1942.
Back cover: Wartime austerity dictated that nothing should be wasted.

British Library Cataloguing-in Publication Data.
A catalogue record for this book is available from the British Library.

ISBN 978-0-9539392-5-1

Published by Finsbury Publishing, 2 Harvest Close, Telscombe Cliffs, Peacehaven, East Sussex BN10 7JG

Contents

Sussex Street, bombed on 29th March, 1943. (Brighton History Centre)

Introduction

New Year's Day, 1942: the war had now entered its fourth year, and the people had well and truly settled into the routine of rationing, austerity and air raids. They looked back to 1941 and saw that there were not so many air attacks on Brighton and Hove as there had been in 1940, when deaths and casualties were high. Would there be even fewer in 1942?

The threat of an invasion by the German military forces was well beyond worry, and some people were even thinking about the Allied forces invading Europe, although that would be a little way off yet. However, not all residents celebrating the coming of another year would be seeing its ending. Some serious air attacks were about to happen, while as far as Brighton and Hove were concerned 1943 would prove even worse.

The month of January started as 1941 had finished. During the morning of January 1st two Messerschmitt 109s attacked a train and

A small tank known as a Waltzing Matilda on display in the grounds of the Royal Pavilion towards the end of the war. (Brighton History Centre)

Staff at the Zylo Works in Richmond Street during a VIP visit. (David Maltby, Zylo Works)

a number of buildings at Rye, while a man was killed in a fishing boat off Hastings. Sites across the county were attacked with a high degree of accuracy, with bombs being dropped on strategic targets as well as the civilian population.

The first bit of real excitement occurred during the night of 7th-8th May when a Heinkel He111 of 7/KG100 was shot down by Squadron Leader Topham and Flying Officer Berridge in a Beaufighter of 219 Squadron, crashing into high powered cables at Patcham and killing all on board. The remains of the aircraft brought hundreds of sightseers rushing to the scene as news got around.

The first air attack on Brighton occurred in the early hours of Tuesday 1st June when a number of bombs were dropped and they all landed harmlessly in fields in the Moulscoomb area. On the 26th Marine Gate was attacked by two low flying Messerschmitt 109s with their cannons and machine guns. They returned again on the 29th August, and this time a woman was killed in the flats.

The worst air attack of 1942 was on 12th October when several bombs were dropped in the Seven Dials and Preston Circus areas. This resulted in a number of deaths and other casualties including a two-year-old boy. Rottingdean suffered its first and only air attack a week before Christmas, on 18th December.

Meanwhile Hove went more than six months before the enemy aircraft attacked the town. At 6.40am on the 27th July four bombs were dropped in the sea close to the foreshore. A total of just six air attacks occurred on Hove during this year, all considered minor. No members of the civilian population lost their lives.

During 1943, however, Brighton suffered two of its three major air attacks, and possibly the worst. February 13th would see the raiders in the area once more, when a number of bombs fell on grassland close to Crescent Drive South in Woodingdean. In March the municipal clinic was bombed, resulting in many deaths, but the worst air attack occurred on 25th May, when the skies above the town were filled with enemy aircraft and their bombs. The railway viaduct crossing

Testing an air raid siren, used to warn the public of an impending raid. These tests were carried out at regular intervals throughout the war. (Brighton History Centre)

Testing a tank (possibly a Matilda) in Preston Park during 1944. This was part of the training for D Day. (Author's collection)

Preston Road was targeted and Marine Gate was hit by several bombs, a number of which passed through the building.

St Cuthman's Church, Whitehawk, suffered a direct hit in August, killing a warden who was on duty there. October saw another bomb cause damage to the railway when a large bomb fell in the cutting behind Bonchurch Road. This would be the last air attack of 1943. The attackers would return in March of the following year, when again the target was the East Brighton area, and many deaths were caused in Bennett Road. Two minor air attacks occurred in 1944 with no casualties.

What of Hove? It would suffer only six air attacks in 1943, but this was nevertheless a very grim year for the town, with disastrous casualties – a total of 20 civilian deaths as well as two servicemen killed and almost 70 people injured. The two worst air attacks occurred on March 9th and 29th.

In 1944 there were just two more attacks by enemy aircraft, and the towns would look forward to the D-Day landings in June of that year. By the following May Europe would once again be free.

David Rowland
Telscombe Cliffs, 2007

Warship Week

Throughout the war years just about every city, town and village was asked to raise money for the war effort, and in particular to buy arms, ships and aeroplanes. The general public were encouraged to part with their money under the guise of terms like Spitfire Fund and Wings Day.

One of the famous weeks that occurred locally and became a massive success was Warship Week. Brighton, Hove and Southwick all organised a fund aimed at raising money for the Navy. Exhibitions, talks and other events were arranged to raise money, no matter how small the sum turned out to be.

Brighton were being extremely ambitious and decided to raise a huge sum, having a target of £700,000. The sum was being raised under the guise of adopting *HMS Kipling*. This ship was a 'K' class destroyer and built in 1939, being commanded by Tony St. Clair Ford.

This momentous week of saving began on Saturday the 7th February 1942, and the local newspapers gave it enormous publicity. Sir Patrick Hastings and George Hicks MP, who were both described as being 'very witty' speakers, made their way through large crowds for the official opening of the campaign at the Corn Exchange in Church Street at 12 noon.

The object was to make the public 'savings conscious'. They encouraged everyone to save anything from 6d upwards, and it was explained that various savings centres would be opened throughout the town during the coming week. Savings bonds, national war bonds, defence bonds and savings certificates were on sale, as well as Post Office or Trustee savings. Those responsible wanted to ensure that the public would watch the total

Nelson's Column comes to Brighton. A group of firemen at Preston Circus built it by their fire station, with a chart showing how much money was raised for Warship Week.

rise and would be kept fully aware of all that was happening. They wanted local people to be involved as much as possible: just about every speaker made this point. To keep them fully aware and interested at all times, the organisers came up with a novel indicator. A replica of Nelson's Column was erected in the centre of Preston Circus. This column was topped by a life size figure of Nelson, and the height of the structure rose to 53 feet

The column was built by a group of firemen from the nearby fire station in their own time, a wonderful thing admired by everyone who saw it. The firemen responsible for the building of it included Stan Ridge, Harry Trott and Anthony Stoner. Then there were Tommy Hume and Frank Woods, who created the decorative artwork and signs. Mention must be made of Rob White, who took care of the slogans and posters. A smaller savings indicator was placed in Castle Square.

Never say die spirit: a newspaper appeal for cash to replace HMS Kipling.

As Saturday came to an end the amount that the public had saved was an incredible £81,991, and as the week progressed the sum of money recorded continued to rise. By the end of Thursday it had reached £609,788 – a magnificent total, especially when you think of what wages were at that time.

A trolley bus was decorated and used as a mobile selling centre, and it travelled on all the Brighton bus routes assisting in the sale of savings certificates and savings stamps. The total raised on the bus was £1,719.3s.2d. with still one day left to complete the week. 'Warship Week badges' were also sold from the bus, and that raised another £80, these two amounts being added to the main total. By the end of the week the total raised exceeded more than £2,000.

A fleet of 'Stop me and buy one' tricycles was used as mobile selling centres, these being used by relays of boys from Brighton College in Eastern Road. Their contributions raised a little over £200 in the sale of savings stamps, one of the officials remarking that it was 'a wonderful effort.'

Meanwhile in Hove, the target was £425,000 – the cost of a submarine. The final total exceeded that target by £1,127. Thereafter the town adopted the submarine *HMS Unbeaten*.

In Southwick 'Warship Week' resulted in investments totalling more than £58,000. The chairman of the urban district council, George Coultrup, thanked all those who had worked tirelessly for the magnificent effort and especially mentioned those gallant members of the WVS.

In July 1942, it was announced that *HMS Kipling*, the ship that the town 'adopted' by the residents of Brighton, had been sunk. This news had a profound effect on the whole of the town, percolating with great sadness especially among those who had recently worked so hard to raise the money a few short weeks before.

The commander of the ship, Anthony St. Clair Ford, came to Brighton and explained in fine detail the story of what happened. He said that the ship had been sunk during the battle for Crete when German Stuka aircraft attacked them, sometimes being between six and 10 aircraft attacking at any one time. There were U-boats involved in the battle, and *HMS Kipling* had just picked up a number of survivors from two torpedoed ships. At that time it was carrying

HMS Cockade was adopted by Brighton in 1943 to replace HMS Kipling, lost during a battle at sea.

around 300 survivors as well as their own crew. They were making their way back to Alexandria when they too were attacked and bombed. During the battle they managed to sink one of the attacking U-Boats and then rescued 31 German survivors, who thus became prisoners of war. A destroyer which was also involved in the battle then rescued all those being carried by *HMS Kipling*, a total of 600 men.

Brighton decided that they would attempt to raise another £700,000 for a new destroyer – *HMS Cockade*. A new campaign was quickly organised and by the 25th July 1942 they had reached the sum of £423,760. It had already been recognised that they would not be able to raise the target in a week as had happened last time, but they did agree that they would keep collecting until the target was reached. On the Monday of each week the organisers would rally their workers to keep pushing for the money and the target was eventually achieved on 5th September.

It was almost unbelievable that this amount should be raised once again so soon after the first effort. It was truly a case of 'Very well done, Brighton!'

The Civic Restaurant

The first Civic Restaurant in Brighton was opened in London Road on 11th May, 1942. The restaurant occupied the ground floor of what was a furniture shop on the west side of London Road almost opposite the Co-op store. Time and money had been spent on the restaurant and this had made room for some 250 seats at the square tables with ample space between them. Provision had been made for the upper part of the old furniture shop to be transformed as an extension to the downstairs seating capacity. The premises had deliberately been given an airy and light feel, and the chairs, of a reddish hue, were very comfortable. The tables, seating four, had white table clothes and a vase of flowers. Loudspeakers provided the music.

The restaurant had been inaugurated with the approval of the Ministry of Food, which had provided all the equipment. The restaurant worked on the cafeteria principle, with each customer taking a tray at the entrance and being served at the metal counter by staff made up of workers from voluntary groups – mainly from the WVS, who seemed to enjoy the work. They were happy and jovial women and always so helpful. They sincerely believed that they were helping the war effort by being able to feed so many people.

It was open for the service of dinners between 12 noon and 2pm, daily except Sundays. However, in case of emergencies the hours would be extended and then it would be open all day including Sundays.

The first meal served on the opening day consisted of roast beef, yorkshire pudding, potatoes and greens followed by rice pudding. A two-course dinner cost 11d. A cup of tea was an extra 1d, while a slice of bread cost a halfpenny.

On Saturday, 16th May the restaurant received a visit from Lord Woolton, the food minister. His first words to the mayor, Alderman Huggett, as he finished his inspection was, 'You look as if you are ready for anything.'

Outside the restaurant were emergency feeding units, which he also inspected. The restaurant was crowded with diners when he arrived, accompanied by Lady Woolton and a number of officials and digniataries. Lord Woolton patted the head of a small boy and asked him if he was enjoying his pudding and when Councillor Miss Stringer told the mother of his identity the news quickly spread that the food minister was in the restaurant, and this led to a hearty round of applause.

Lord Woolton made a thorough inspection of the restaurant and spent some time behind the counter watching the serving of the meals. He then went outside to inspect the mobile food vans. Just before he left, he told the mayor that he was thoroughly satisfied with the arrangements made by Brighton for communal and emergency feeding and was very pleased with what he had seen.

As Lord Woolton made his way to his car, a woman in the crowd said to him, 'Thank you for all you have done for us.' Smiling, he acknowledged the greeting, mouthing the words, 'Thank you.'

Before Lord Woolton had arrived, Mr. Midgely of Messrs. Hartley and Midgely officially handed over to the mayor two emergency

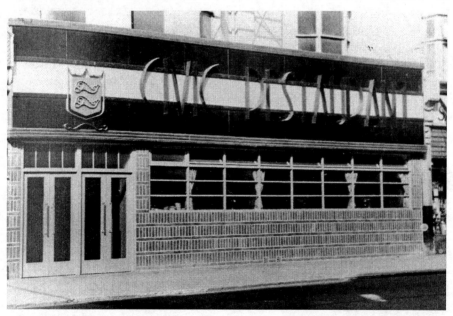

The Civic Restaurant, opposite the Co-op, served cheap meals. It closed in 1945. (Brighton History Centre)

feeding units presented by the car manufacturer Henry Ford and his son, Edsel B. Ford. The vans were fitted with insulated containers and equipment necessary to serve hot food to 640 people and were provided for the purpose of carrying hot food to agricultural workers, school children and other civilian workers who, through stress of war, required hot meals. They also carried hot food from central kitchens or cooking depots to British restaurants or feeding centres. This arrangement could be extended by taking food direct to people who brought their own dishes and carried it away to eat in their own homes – an early 'take-away'. They became in effect mobile 'British restaurants', staffed by members of the WVS and other voluntary workers. The local vans were voluntarily maintained by Hartley and Midgely, and took their place in Brighton's 'wartime meals service', with similar vehicles that had already been presented to the town by people of Southern Rhodesia, Brighton in Pennsylvania, Jamaica and the Lord Mayor of London's air raid fund. All of these vehicles were used after bombing incidents until the end of the war.

In January of 1944 consideration was given to the Civic Restaurant opening for longer hours. It was decided to open during the evenings on a trial basis, and this began at the beginning of February. A report in the *Brighton and Hove Herald* on 11th March, 1944, revealed that things were not always under control. What was officially described as 'A display of an excessive exuberance of spirit by young visitors to the Civic Restaurant during evening hours of opening,' resulted in the exclusion from the premises of all young people under the age of 16, unless their parents accompanied them.

When the facilities of the restaurant were first made available for evenings it was never intended that it should be used to any extent by children. The principle idea was that it would be a centre where young men and women could get refreshment and, if desired, participate in games. Gradually children made their appearance in ever increasing numbers and, a spokesman said, 'as invariably happens when boys gather together, they become somewhat noisy, bubbling over with youthful spirit'.

Mr. Avery, the wartime meals officer for Brighton said, 'There has been larking about, but nothing in the nature of stand-up fighting. No crockery has been thrown about and no one has been thrown out.

Since the restaurant opened in the evening it has gradually become busier and today there are some 200 people using it every evening.'

On the 5th March, however, a doorkeeper was introduced in order to stop children under the age of 16 from going inside.

Mr. Holloway, a local youth organiser, said that he took strong exception to suggestions that there had been any rowdyism at the restaurant, when in fact all that happened was a display of high spirits.

WARTIME HUMOUR

Soon after a bomb had fallen and the rescuers were hard at work digging through the rubble of one of the bombed houses they heard the sound of laughter. They stopped to listen and they heard a man laughing uncontrollably.

'Poor devil,' they thought. 'He must be hysterical.'

They continued with their digging and eventually dug their way through to him. They found him sitting on the toilet covered in dust and rubble, but still laughing his head off.

'Are you all right, mate?' they asked.

'Yes,' came the reply.

'Why are you laughing so much?'

'Well,' he said, 'I'd just finished, and so I stood up. I pulled the chain and the ruddy house fell down.'

Tragedy in Rottingdean

At about 10pm on Wednesday 29th July 1942, the body of a young girl was found dead in her bedroom by her family. Ellen Short lived with her parents and her two sisters at 55, Marine Drive, Rottingdean – a 'refreshment house' run by her parents on the coast road near the Rottingdean crossroads.

She was 22-years-old, very attractive, and had been going out with Charles Stenning for about six years. Charles, who lived at 13, Apollo Terrace in Brighton, had taken up an apprenticeship as a plumber with a local firm when he left school

When the war came Charles Stenning joined the navy, his service number being P/M/X 78066. By mid 1942 and aged 21, he had been promoted to petty officer (plumber) and was stationed at Portsmouth. This was a good posting for him, as it was a fairly easy journey by train to Brighton, although on most occasions he hitch-hiked. He was so in love with Ellen (who was known as 'Nellie') that after joining the navy he had tattooed her name and a heart on his right arm, so that he would not forget the girl he left behind.

At the end of July he was home on leave, and on Wednesday the 29th his first task was to go to Rottingdean. However, unbeknown to him, Ellen had met a Canadian soldier, Frederick Cathcart, who was stationed in Brighton, and on this day he had called at the house to see her. It was evening time and although her parents were out, her sister Eileen was at home.

When Charles arrived he was shocked to see Ellen and Cathcart together. All three of them were in the house for a short while before Cathcart left. Stenning was terribly upset and couldn't understand what was going on. The words between them got more and more heated, as her sister later testified, and after a while Ellen ran upstairs to her bedroom in floods of tears. She wanted Charles to leave.

He sat downstairs for a few minutes and then followed her upstairs to her bedroom. There, it seems, it became clear to him that their romance was over. This was the last straw for him: he just couldn't face life without her.

In the bedroom was a knobbed article that was something like the handle of a leather riding stick. In a fit of rage he struck her on the head with it, then strangled her with a stocking tied tightly around her neck. He then left the house.

Her father later went upstairs and found Ellen murdered in the bedroom. He called the police, who quickly circulated Stenning's description – 5' 8" tall, slight build, bronzed complexion with a long face and good teeth.

On Friday morning, a man answering Stenning's description was seen on the cliff top at Peacehaven by two policemen. He was sitting near the edge of the cliffs at Friars Bay. He got up and started walking towards them, but when they were within fifty yards, he apparently saw them, turned, ran and jumped over the cliff edge.

When the body was recovered, it was found to be that of Charles Stenning, in his naval uniform.

On examining the spot on the cliff top where he had been sitting, the officers found his pay book and Post Office savings bank book lying on the grass. They were alongside a copy of the *Sussex Daily News*, open at the page reporting the girl's death.

A Canadian officer was lowered down the 150 feet cliff and managed to secure a rope around the body. Two other Canadian soldiers brough up the body, and then the officer was hauled up. An incoming tide made it imperative to recover the body before the tide took it out to sea.

The inquest

The inquest was held the following Wednesday, 5th August, in Brighton by the coroner, Charles Webb. The exhibits on show included a blood stained stocking and the knobbed article, described as a cosh.

Dr. Eileen Wood, who examined the body, stated that she found a wound on the neck about one inch long, and two small cuts branching from it. The head wound, probably caused by the cosh, did not contribute towards her death.

PC Alfred Potten, of the East Sussex Constabulary and stationed at Peacehaven, said in evidence that at about 11am on Friday 31st July he and PC Kirby were inspecting unoccupied premises at

Peacehaven when he saw a man sitting on the grass promenade about eight yards from the cliff edge. He was reading a newspaper. The man turned round and seeing the police, dropped the newspaper and ran to the edge of the cliff and jumped over.

Detective Superintendent Pelling told the inquest, 'I went to the second floor bedroom at the Midget Stores, Marine Drive, Rottingdean, where I found the body of the dead girl. The bedclothes were blood-stained and the rugs on the floor were in disorder.'

He produced a letter from Charles Stenning, dated 29th July at 1.15am and addressed to Cathcart.

Superintendent Pelling continued. 'I would like to mention the appreciation of the police of the services of Lieutenant Lloyd and several Canadian NCOs. They rendered valuable assistance in bringing up the body of Stenning from the foot of the cliffs to the top. The cliff top was concave and it was a very difficult operation. Two of the men in particular went to considerable personal risk to themselves in actually bringing up the body. Stenning had died from a fractured skull.

Detective Constable Arthur Wilkinson produced photographs, which he had taken of the dead girl and of the room. The jury expressed their admiration of these photographs

Friars Bay, Peacehaven, pictured in 2003.

15

The coroner said Stenning's letter was a long one and that it was only necessary to refer to excerpts. One part read, 'I guess you will be very surprised to hear from me, but I think we have a few things to settle between us. One thing, I must tell you, is that Nellie means more than anything else in the world . . . ' (The words 'to me' had been written next, said the coroner, but had been struck out. They should be read with the context to make the meaning clear.)

The letter continued, 'and I would rather lose my right arm than see her unhappy. Nellie means so much to me that I would rather see her happy with another guy than unhappy with me.'

'You will see' went on the coroner, 'the sense of the letter is that Stenning was jealous of Cathcart but was willing to stand aside if he was assured that Cathcart and the girl could be happy together.'

Towards the end of the hearing, Mr John Short, the dead girl's father stood up and asked to be allowed to say a few words. He said, 'We have known him (Stenning) for six years and have seen a lot of him. We had the highest opinion of him. I have never seen him in a bad temper, he was always most sociable and I never heard him quarrel.'

Robert Todd, the foreman, announced the jury's verdict, that Ellen Short was murdered by Charles Stenning and that Stenning took his own life while the balance of his mind was disturbed.

He added, 'The jury would like to say how deeply they sympathise with the relatives in both cases.'

Marine Gate Flats

At about 2.15pm on the afternoon of Saturday 29th August, 1942, two enemy aircraft flew low across the Channel and attacked the block of flats on the cliff top known as Marine Gate. The residents and military alike had little time to prepare to take shelter as the planes strafed the building and nearby residential properties.

The enemy aircraft, almost certainly Focke-Wulf 190s, carried a bomb under each aircraft, and they attacked the flats because they believed they were a military hospital. It would surely have been rather strange to have a hospital in such a prominent position, but perhaps they thought it was a case of 'double bluff'.

The aircraft dropped their two bombs close to the flats, causing major damage and the death of one resident, 20-year-old Claudette Mawby. Claudette was one of three sisters famous for appearing in films around that time.

The Marine Gate flats after the raid in August 1942 in which a young woman died.

The attack, as usual for this type of 'sneak' raid, lasted seconds, but the clearing up would last for days and weeks. Marine Gate was not only badly damaged by the two bombs but had been strafed with machine gun and canon fire. Many of the flats had suffered internal damage, with doors ripped from their hinges and dozens of broken windows, the glass scattered in small pieces around the building.

The rescue services were soon on hand and, together with the National Fire Service, soon had the two small fires under control. The injured, three seriously, were taken to the Royal Sussex County hospital.

The final repairs were still being carried out when the building was again seriously damaged in May 1943.

The Clinic Raid

One of Brighton's worst air raids occurred on Monday 29th March 1943. The day started with hazy sunshine but started to cloud over towards the end of the morning.

The School Clinic was situated on the corner of Ivory Place and opposite the fruit and vegetable market in Circus Street. Soon after 11am it was very busy with a number of children visiting the dentist and expectant mothers attending the pre-natal clinic.

The sirens sounded their mournful warning, and at about the same time enemy aircraft were overhead. The sound of people screaming as they rushed for shelter could plainly be heard. Four Focke-Wulf 190s started to machine-gun the streets as they flew low over the town. On their second run they dropped their bombs, each one of 500kg. One struck the rooftop of a terraced house in William Street, which caused it to deflect and act as a torpedo. The bomb entered the southern end of the fruit and vegetable market and

Rescue workers taking a break at a WVS van. Similar vehicles attended all serious bombings and rescues. (Author's collection)

travelled the whole length before bursting out at the northern end, crossing the road and exploding near the front entrance of the clinic. The blast from the explosion caused the deaths of two children. People were buried in the debris.

Meanwhile another bomb fell and exploded nearby in Gloucester Place, partly demolishing the Baptist church and some tenement buildings. This bomb caused further deaths and extensive damage.

A third bomb fell in Grosvenor Street, a street of terraced houses, and again causing death and destruction. As was often the case, there were the 'lucky' escapes. A boy home from school as he was feeling unwell was lying in the family's Morrison shelter when his house was struck. The shelter was covered with debris and rubble from the house but he managed to be rescued with no injuries, although he was badly shaken.

The rescue services were soon on the scene, ably assisted by Canadian soldiers who were stationed in the town together with a number of sailors. Ambulances were kept very busy ferrying the wounded to the two local hospitals. The ambulance crews were most grateful when two army ambulances joined in and ferried a number of injured people to the Royal Sussex County Hospital. The bodies of the dead were taken to the mortuary in Park Street.

The raid barely took more than two minutes as the enemy aircraft started to make their escape. However a spitfire was on patrol and was soon vectored towards Brighton. He made for one of the Focke-Wulf 190s and shot it down. The enemy aircraft crashed into the sea about a half mile south of the Palace pier and sank almost straight away. The pilot was later washed up along the coast and afforded a military funeral in the Bear Road cemetery.

Meanwhile around the same time four other Focke-Wulf 190s were attacking Hove and also caused a number of deaths as well as severe damage.

In Brighton the final death toll was 18 civilians and the German pilot. A large number of people suffered severe injuries and were treated in hospital. Once again first aid stations were set up, and the people with minor injuries were treated there.

Baptist Church, Gloucester Place

Just after 11am on Monday 29th March 1943 four Focke-Wulf 190s of 10/JG54 flew across the Channel at wave height and as they crossed the coastline rose to a height of some 200ft before dropping their bombs and machine-gunning the town.

They had left their base at St. Omer-Wizernes about twenty minutes earlier. Their leader, Obrlt. Paul Keller had been killed some four days earlier when his Focke-Wulf 190A-5 had been hit by anti-aircraft fire and exploded in the air over Ashford, Kent. Their new leader, Oberlt. Erwin Busch, had been given orders to attack first Brighton, dropping their bombs in the town centre, and then Hove. He had told the listening pilots to use their machine guns and and canons to cause as much fear as they could.

Uffz. Joachim Koch had listened intently to these instructions. Just before 11am he had climbed into his Focke-Wulf 190A-5, Werk no. 2576, and within a couple of minutes he and his companions were airborne and heading towards Brighton on their deadly

Gloucester Place Baptist church, 29th March, 1943.

Above: Another view of the rescue operation at the Baptist church.

Below: Richmond Buildings. On the left of the photograph is St Peter's church hall, where the Baptist congregation held its meetings after the bombing.

mission. He wasn't to know that he had little more than twenty minutes of his life remaining.

The coastal defences opened fire as the four enemy aircraft approached, but the Germans caught the seafront guns napping due to their low altitude.

They circled the town before they made their bomb run, aiming for anywhere in the centre of Brighton. It was thought that they deliberately aimed for the clinic, but that was not true, for almost as soon as they started their bomb run two Spitfires of 610 Squadron were on to them. They had been engaged in a photography exercise and happened to be in the area. One Spitfire, flown by Flying Officer Francois Venesoen, attacked Koch's Focke-Wulf, shooting it down into the sea about 500 yards south of the Palace Pier. Another Focke-Wulf was shot down into the sea, but a German patrol boat rescued the pilot, who was uninjured.

One of the bombs passed through the Brighton fruit and vegetable market in Circus Street, travelling like a torpedo. It had been dropped through the market from south to north, bursting out through the wall and crossing the roadway before exploding close to the entrance of the municipal clinic.

Another bomb fell about 100 yards away, hitting a tall tenement building and an adjoining Baptist church. This caused loss of life and serious damage. The Baptist church was almost cut in half. The town around the St.Peter's church area was plunged into mayhem, as dozens of people had run for shelter as the aircraft appeared overhead. However, as often happened on these air attacks, it was all over in seconds with the enemy aircraft gone and the town left with fires, debris and clouds of dust and dirt everywhere. A bus driving northwards along Gloucester Place had stopped as the driver heard the first explosion together with the machine gun fire, thus saving many lives since the blast from the bomb in Gloucester Place would almost certainly have added to the list of casualties. The only person injured was the conductor, who slipped, hurting her back, as the vehicle suddenly stopped.

In Hove, bombs fell in Nizells Avenue, Shirley Street, Colbourne Road and Clarenden Villas. Nine people were killed, 17 were seriously injured and 34 people suffered what were described as 'slight injuries.' The Baptist church in Gloucester Place was set on fire, but with the aid of the fire service the flames were soon brought under control. This did add to the damage already caused by the bomb, and those people responsible for the church were reduced to tears on seeing what had happened to it.

They returned the following morning, having digested the damage and its consequences in terms of rebuilding. Their minister had had previous experience of both church and home bombing in the London blitz, and was therefore very much on familiar ground when dealing with the emergencies, but many years were to elapse before the congregation were able to clear the debt.

On the morning after the raid the vicar of St. Peter's church offered the Baptists the loan of the small church hall in Richmond Buildings as a temporary place of worship. The kind offer was gladly accepted, and the Baptists thus found themselves able to worship in comfortable although unaccustomed surroundings. The minister of a strict Baptist chapel in Brighton later offered the full use of its premises. The Baptists were very much touched by the practical sympathy which their loss had aroused.

The Worst Raid on Brighton

It was a very pleasant morning on the 25th May 1943 as people made their way to work and children started to get ready for school.

The talk of those days was still the terrible bombing of the school clinic in March, when a number of people had been killed. That had been the first bombing raid for some time, and people had begun to believe that the attacks were perhaps coming to an end.

The first warning of impending danger came around 12.20pm when, simultaneously with the air raid siren sounding, the skies over the town were full of German aircraft. It seemed to onlookers at that time that there were hundreds of them. In fact there were just 25 Focke-Wulf 190s, but almost all of them were carrying large bombs, and Brighton and Hove were definitely the targets.

The aircraft swooped low over the town. Some had crossed the coastline near Roedean and formed up to the north of the town before coming into their targets at Black Rock and Marine Gate. They scored a direct hit on the gasworks and several hits on the Marine Gate flats, with some bombs actually passing through the building. The miracle of this raid was that no one was killed in the flats at

A bomb struck one of the piers of the railway viaduct in Preston Road, Brighton, and the blast damaged houses nearby. (Robert Ellison)

Smashed railway coaches near Brighton railway station after the raid of 25th May, 1943. (Robert Ellison)

Marine Gate, although the bomb that struck the gasometers caused serious damage to St. Mark's school nearby and three people were killed, including two policemen who were on duty close by.

Other bombs fell in a number of locations throughout the town causing widespread damage and a number of deaths. This raid is probably best known for the damage done to the railway viaduct in Preston Road. The bomb that struck the viaduct took down one of the support pillars putting the eastern rail link out of action for a few weeks. Another bomb struck a small parade of shops in Down Terrace, again causing death and serious inury. The rescue services were at full stretch and help was called for from Hove and Portslade. These workers did sterling work and were well complimented on in the days that followed.

Once again the eastern part of the town was the worst hit, as bombs caused damage and mayhem in the Kemp Town area. Rescues were undertaken in Eastern Road and Chichester Place, rescuing people and recovering a number of bodies. Meanwhile a tragedy was unfolding in Bennett Road where one of the occupants, Mrs Avis, had sought the relative safety of her Morrison shelter in her ground floor front room. One of the large bombs struck the house and the blast blew the shelter with Mrs Avis inside right down her garden, past a garden on the next street and into the rear of a house. The shelter broke up and Mrs. Avis was found lying dead against the wall of the house.

A large number of Canadian troops were stationed in Brighton at this time and one such unit was based in St. Mary's Hall. They soon were mobilised and took part in the rescues in that part of town. A number of first aid post were set up and before long large queues of people with minor injuries were patiently standing in line for treatment. Meanwhile, hospital staff struggled to treat the more seriously injured, and many people had to wait a long time before it became their turn to be seen.

The official figures state that 24 people lost their lives including two young children, while another 130 people needed hospital treatment. This was by far the town's worst raid in regard to the numbers of aircraft attacking the town and the damage done. It took the townspeople a long time to make good the damage caused on this day, and those who lost family members would never get over it.

• The author tells a full and more detailed story of this air raid in his book *Out of the Blue*, also published by Finsbury.

Grosvenor Street, off Edward Street, after the raid. (Author's collection)

GOEBBELS HECKLED IN ESSEN

Goebbels was greeted with 'You caused all this' when he visited Essen after a recent raid, according to reports from Germany that reached the Swedish newspaper Arbetet.

The broad mass of the people, say travellers reaching Sweden, feel that they are merely harvesting what the Luftwaffe has sown – reported by Reuters in Stockholm yesterday.

– Sussex Daily News, Friday 4th June, 1943

St Cuthman's church, Whitehawk

It was just after 12.15am on Monday 16th August 1943 that German aircraft were heard overhead. The sirens had sounded a couple of minutes before and many people were safely in their shelters. It was suggested at the time that these enemy aircraft were returning from a raid and were heading back across the Channel when one aircraft dropped three bombs that landed in Whitehawk. One landed on playing fields in Whitehawk Road, at the foot of the Race Hill, another to the east of Wilson Avenue, causing a large crater, while the third one scored a direct hit on St. Cuthman's church at the junction of Lintott Avenue and Fletching Road.

The bomb caused extensive damage to the church, destroying the beautiful organ, the roof and two outer walls, and part of the church collapsed, leaving just the tower standing.

St Cuthman's in Lintott Avenue after a bomb scored a direct hit. An air raid warden on duty inside the building was killed. (Author's collection)

HERALD

SATURDAY, AUGUST 21, 1943

The occupants of this house—including three little children—had just taken shelter when a block of masonry from the church which was damaged during Monday's raid crashed through the side of the bedroom where they had been sleeping. They were all unhurt.

In the church hall, which doubled as an air raid warden's post, was William Hayler. He died while writing out his warden's report sheet. Half of the church hall was demolished and rescuers found a scattered pack of cards, a dust-covered billiards table and torn magazines among a pile of rubble. This is all that remained of the warden's post that took up around half of the hall. Strangely the other half was not badly damaged. Sadly, Mr. Hayler was not due to work that night but had swapped shifts in order to do a favour for a friend, another of the wardens team.

Mr. Hayler, who was engaged in war work at the Allen West factory, was a keen gardener and worked an allotment. After his death, two of his friends carried on with his allotment and sold the produce to raise a little money for his widow. On the 23rd September, the wardens and their friends put on a concert at Whitehawk Boys School to raise more money for Mr. Hayler's widow and family. This concert was well attended and a tidy sum of money was handed over a few days later.

A number of houses in the immediate vicinity were badly damaged and number of residential and business properties suffered slight damage, mainly consisting of roof damage and broken windows.

A number of people had lucky escapes, among them a Mrs Cole who lived close-by with her seven year old son, Raymond, and her mother, Mrs. Weller. As the sirens sounded they left their bedroom for the Morrison table shelter, and when they returned to the bedroom after the 'All clear' had sounded they found that a large block of masonry from the church had crashed through the wall, leaving a gaping hole at the back of the bed. (See the photograph on the opposite page.)

The following day the vicar, Reverend Chris Bryan was interviewed by the local press.

'As I am a part-time warden,' he said, 'I was already dressed and coming down the stairs when the bomb fell. My wife was in the vicarage, which is only a few feet away from the north-west side of the church. We heard nothing at this time to suggest that the bomb had dropped within a few yards of us. You can imagine my consternation therefore when I opened the door and saw a heap of rubble where the church had stood.

'It is noteworthy,' the vicar added, 'that although the church was practically demolished, the tower bearing a gilt cross was left standing. And although almost everything inside was damaged, the large crucifix behind the altar remained in position and escaped without a scratch. Except for slight damage to the roof and one or two cracked panes of glass, the vicarage escaped damage.'

The vicar and his helpers were at work early the morning after the bomb fell, salvaging everything that was possible to pick up.

Temporary arrangements were made for services to be held in the vicarage. However, by the following Sunday the congregation was established at St. David's Hall, in Whitehawk Avenue at its junction with Whitehawk Road. The newspaper reported a few days later that no attempt had yet been made to clear away the wreckage of the church, and the vicar pointed out that local authorities were not allowed to touch ecclesiastical property without special government sanction.

NOTE FROM THE MEDIA FOR 1943

It was announced in the Brighton and Hove Herald on the 9th January 1943 that the OBE had been awarded to the town clerk, Mr J.G.Drew. He was appointed in 1938 but from 1939 until 1942 he was the ARP Controller for the town before resigning and resuming his town clerk duties. Hearty congratulations were afforded from the town council as well as from many well-wishers.

On 5th February 1943 King George of the Hellenes (Greece) made a surprise and unofficial visit to Brighton with some friends. He visited Mr. Berry Harding's well known 'Harlequin' antique shop in a picturesque corner of Kings Road.

His majesty particularly liked a pair of coloured statues of Queen Victoria and Prince Albert. His interest was further heightened by the knowledge that Queen Mary had visited this quaint shop, a survivor of the 17th century, in pre-war days.

The deputy chief constable of Sussex Police, Captain W.J. Hutchinson, was awarded the King's Police Medal in the birthday honours list. He had followed his father and grandfather into the police service.

The 'unilateral' system for 'waiting' traffic was first introduced at Brighton under Captain Hutchinson. It is also interesting to note that the police pocket wireless system was developed to a high state of efficiency under his guidance. He wrote two textbooks that became standard volumes throughout police circles.

A number of town dignitaries were at Brighton railway station to see 80 local children being evacuated on Tuesday 6th July. They were mostly girls, and they travelled in two parties to start a new life in Yorkshire. The children, whose ages ranged from 5 years old to 14, were members of 44 families. They were bound for five reception areas from where they were conducted to their journey's end.

Bonchurch Road

At about 3.45am on Friday 22nd October 1943 the residents of Bonchurch Road and the surrounding area were awakened from their slumbers by the screaming sound of a diving enemy aircraft from the cloudy night sky. The sirens sounded around the same time as the residents scrambled from their beds and hurried to their shelters. Some people hadn't enough time to get out of their beds, while others slept through the whole incident.

However, there was no mistaking the sound of the 500kg bomb exploding in the railway cutting that ran along the back of Bonchurch Road. The enemy aircraft was one of a number crossing the Sussex and Kent coasts en route to London, several of them managing to get through to the City. It was thought that the plane which dropped the bomb (possibly aimed at the railway viaduct) returned to its base without taking the risk of flying to London.

The bomb exploded at the rear of no. 79 and the residents there thought themselves very lucky indeed to only suffer minimal injuries and shock. Thankfully, the high banks of the cutting took the worst of the blast of the bomb and the damage was mainly to

The rear of the houses in Bonchurch Road after a bomb exploded in the railway cutting. As many as 870 houses were damaged. (Brighton History Centre)

The railway cutting at the rear of Bonchurch Road after the bomb fell. Houses were damaged within a radius of half a mile. (Brighton History Centre)

windows and roofs of the nearby houses, athough eleven people suffered minor injuries. Only three of them needed to go to the hospital in Elm Grove to receive treatment, while the other eight were treated by first aid teams. One child was among those who attended hospital, injured when the ceiling of her bedroom fell on her.

The houses nearest to the impact suffered the most from the blast, and a number of roofs and ceilings collapsed covering those still in their beds with a liberal layer of dust, dirt and debris.

Almost all of the rear windows of the nearby Elm Grove School were broken and the school had a certain amount of roof damage. The children found to their absolute delight that they were forced to take a short holiday while the school was being repaired.

The Sunny Bank Laundry at nos. 82–84, suffered very serious

damage, the top part of the building being all but demolished. There were no people on the premises at this time.

Houses in Seville Street and Wellington Street were also affected, suffering the same type of damage, with smashed windows and broken tiles and slates.

After the raid a number of local residents told their stories. Mrs. Bower, who lived close to the laundry, likened it to an earthquake. Mrs Barnard, who lived a couple of doors away from the exploding bomb, said, 'I thought the plane had been hit and was crashing on us. I dived into the cupboard under the stairs and the whole house shook and seemed to sway backwards and forwards with the force of the explosion. A dense cloud of white dust made it impossible to see anything for a few minutes. My piano was lifted bodily across the room – it was a wonder it didn't play a tune.'

Mrs Phyllis Newcombe (née George) later recalled the incident.

'I was 16 years old in 1943 and worked at Timpson's the shoe shop at 106 London Road. I was living at no. 23a with my parents and when the sirens sounded we rushed to our shelter that was under the

Mrs George, Phyllis Newcombe's mother, sitting in the late 1940s at the spot where the shelter used to be. (Mrs P. Newcombe)

front steps of our home. I hated this shelter and on many occasions my Mum would shout at me and tell me to get into it. I used to say, "If I'm going to die, then I want to be in bed".

'On this particular night, the sirens didn't sound and we didn't get to the shelter. There was an almighty bang and the house shook and the doors were blown off their hinges. I wasn't frightened, but my mother was in a terrible state – she couldn't stop shaking. She told me to stop shaking and I had to tell her that it was her who was shaking.

'She was a member of the ARP service but was made redundant as on every occasion she was called out she just couldn't stop shaking with fear. The head of her section was very gentle about her leaving the ARP service.'

The certificate awarded to Mrs George in recognition of her work during the First World War.

Brighton's Last Air Attack

Brighton's last serious air attack occurred during the night of Wednesday 23rd February, 1944, strangely in the same area where the first one had occurred in July 1940. However this one had more serious consequences in regard to human life.

It was a very cold night and Brightonians had seriously begun to believe that the war was almost finished and with that no more bombs would be falling upon them – after all the last one had fallen on the railway track behind Bonchurch Road some four months before. There had of course been air raid siren warnings, but these were generally regarded as false alarms. On this occasion, therefore, not everyone left their beds and picked their way to the shelters when the sirens sounded. Perhaps they should have done so.

By this time the coastline was better protected both with guns and with faster allied aircraft, and with them came night-time patrols. So was it on this night, when a solitary enemy aircraft became trapped in searchlight beams.

The bombs rained down and causing damage to properties in Bennett Road (which suffered the worst damage and the greatest number of casualties), Rugby Place and Eastern Road.

Several people were killed and extensive damage was caused when a bomb fell on Bennett Road in 1944. (Brighton History Centre)

The Morrison shelter at 19 Bennett Road where a woman and two children were rescued uninjured.

Once again the Morrison shelter came into its own and saved yet more people from death or serious injury. It certainly saved the lives of the four members of the Burnett family who had hurried to their shelter at the first hint of trouble. With their house falling all about them they were rescued without a scratch. A little further away another family, the Dinnages, also under their Morrison shelter, escaped after their house was almost totally destroyed.

The nearby Wilson's laundry in Arundel Road was damaged, the worst affected area being the staff canteen, while a gas main in Arundel Road was fractured and caused a large fire before members from the fire service brought it under control.

Once again the Marine Gate flats suffered some minor damage –

Machinery at Wilson's Laundry in Arundel Road damaged by one of the bombs. (Author's collection)

mainly blast damage to the windows and part of a small retaining wall. The rescue services were soon on the scene and quickly requested help from their colleagues at Hove who attended some 45 minutes later. The rescue was soon under way and a number of people, dazed and hurt, were rescued from beneath the debris of their homes.

Then the bodies began to be recovered. The number soon grew and although every so often a call for 'quiet please' was uttered, it was some hours before a woman in her 60s was rescued. Sadly more and more bodies were pulled free, and in total 11 people lost their lives in the various bombed buildings. In Bennett Road a total of nine people were killed. A desperate rescue took place at no. 35 Bennett Road when groaning was heard from beneath the debris. After a couple of hours two brothers, Harry and John Morley, were pulled from the debris. Harry was dead and John, very seriously injured, was rushed to the Royal Sussex County Hospital where he died the next day. Further along the road at no. 49, a mother aged 70 and her 44 year-old son were both killed. On the other side of the road at no. 24 a married couple, Mr and Mrs. Sherlock, both in their 60s, were killed.

An information centre was set up to help those people whose property and houses had been damaged or lost. At around 8am that morning the builders were on the scene and repairs were started to patch up those houses with the least damage.

Note

It is known that on the night of 22nd–23rd February 185 enemy aircraft took off for bombing missions, and of that number 150 crossed the south coast of England. A full total of losses is not listed, but there are a few aircraft known to have been shot down during this night. One of them crashed down in Sussex: was it the one that dropped its bombs on East Brighton?

This aircraft was a Messerschmitt 410A of 14/KG2 (420463) and was shot down by a Mosquito from 96 Squadron, crashing at Bentley Farm, Framfield in East Sussex soon after midnight. Both crew members were killed and the aircraft was destroyed. The pilot was Uffz. R.Eggers.

A

In the years when our Country

was in mortal danger

J.R.McQUEEN.

who served 1st March 1943 to December 1944.

gave generously of his time and

powers to make himself ready

for her defence by force of arms

and with his life if need be.

George R.I.

THE HOME GUARD

A copy of the certificate presented to J.R. McQueen on the disbandment of the Brighton Home Guard at the end of the war. Mr McQueen served with the 15th Sussex (Brighton) Battalion from 1st March, 1943 until December 1944. His son-in-law, Mr Blaber of Telscombe Cliffs, kindly loaned the certificate to the author along with the letter on the facing page.

Farewell to the Home Guard

When J.R. McQueen left the Home Guard at the end of the war he received the following letter:

"Norfolk House"
Norfolk Terrace
Brighton
December 1944

Dear Mr McQueen,

We have arrived at the parting of the ways. For more than four years, while the country was in danger of invasion, we, in common with nearly two millions of our generation, have stood to arms in her defence. It was our obvious duty: we did it; and we have received the most generous thanks of our King and our Town. The episode is closed.

It remains for me to try to express to you, whom it has been my privilege to command, my feelings of gratitude for the most loyal co-operation, which has been outstanding in your service. Every one of you, whether officer, NCO, or man, has contributed his quota to the common effort, and my task consequently has been rendered simple and pleasurable to a degree.

It is my hope that, while one chapter of our history as a unit is closed, another, equally satisfactory, is about to open and that in our Old Comrades Association, we may carry over into the peace the good comradeship and friendship that have characterised our wartime service. We have all been friends together and there is no reason why these ties, which I for one have valued, should be severed. I extend a most hearty invitation to you all.

Christmas is now upon us; allow me therefore to conclude by wishing you, individually and personally, most cordial good wishes for the festive season (may the next one be even more festive), and all happiness and prosperity in the coming years.

Yours very sincerely,

D.W. Blandford

15TH SUSSEX
(BRIGHTON) BATTALION
HOME GUARD

A Typhoon on Brighton beach following a collision on 26th November, 1944. It is believed to have been escorting Winston Churchill back from Germany.

Anthony Simmonds' Story

During the war years there were very strict regulations on mail being sent around the country. Sending letters abroad posed an even greater problem. This kept the censors very busy, and secrecy increased as the war years went on. This brought about ever more staff being drafted into the government censor's department. They would open thousands upon thousands of letters. Their contents determined what action would be taken: the minimum punishment was just a ticking off, but there could be a court action and, in some cases, a prison sentence.

POSTAL CENSORSHIP.

The communication returned in this cover constitutes a breach of the Defence Regulations. The writer is warned to be more careful in future.

N.B. — The communication will be allowed to proceed if the passage or passages referring to (........) are omitted, and if it is re-posted to the addressee in the usual way.

However, most censored letteres had been written without the writer really thinking about the secrecy of the contents: they were composed in total innocence. One such was sent by Mr. Simmonds, Anthony's father, in June 1944 to his old school friend, Edwin Woodward, who had emigrated to the USA in the 1920s. It mentioned the D-Day landings.

In 1940, when many evacuees were being sent to various parts of the country, Mr. Woodward offered to take the three Simmonds children into his home until the end of the war. This was agreed, and they became very excited by the thought of living in America. However soon after this offer came the tragedy of *The City of Benares*. She was a ship heading for Canada, carrying children being evacuated to Canada, and she was sunk by the enemy in the Atlantic with a huge loss of life. This incident changed any idea that the children would go to the USA.

In 1942 Anthony was 13 years old and his brother Dennis was three years younger. They were fascinated by a broadcast, together with media stories, about Mrs. Churchill launching an appeal for 'Aid to Russia'. At this time Russia was desperately defending the city of Stalingrad over a 15-month period, with the citizens very close to starvation during the terrible Russian winter.

The two brothers debated how they could raise some money to

Anthony Simmonds in his schooldays.

donate to the fund. Tony suggested that they could sell off some of their toys, and so they set up a small stall on the pavement outside their home in Winchester. They had to sort out their things prior to moving to Brighton. They sold all their toys, and the money raised was sent to 10 Downing Street, the prime minister's home.

They went to fetch their toys –mainly cars, vans, buses and so on, all made of tin with solid wheels and a key to wind them up. The prize possession was an 18inch-long tin 'Bluebird' with Malcolm Campbell at the wheel. This toy was rivalled by a camouflaged 'Ack Ack' truck with a gun that fired sparks and with a battery operated searchlight that shone on the ceiling. The largest toy sold was a fort with a drawbridge fixed by two chains complete with lead soldiers and some canons that could be fitted on the battlements: I am sure these would be quite valuable today. They were very sad to see their toys being sold but then consoled themselves when the thought of the use the money would be put to.

Imagine the surprise on the two boys' faces when a few weeks later a letter arrived from no.10 Downing Street. It thanked the boys for their endeavours, and was hand-written by Mrs Churchill herself.

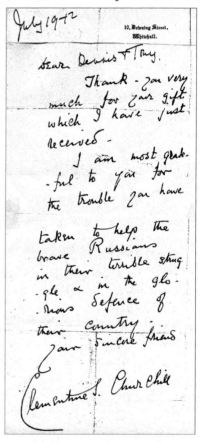

The Brighton Victory Parade

The Brighton Victory Parade took place on Sunday 13th May 1945. The parade lined up on Madeira Drive and at 3.30pm began the march along the seafront to Preston Street.

It included units from the navy, army and air force together with representatives from the local home guard. Members of the police, fire brigade and civil defence as well as pre-service units joined them.

The salute was taken outside the Old Ship Hotel by Brigadier K. Stewart MC, commander of the West Sussex sub-district, supported by the town's mayor.

A similar parade was held in Hove and was lined up in the Drive for inspection before marching off at 2pm to the county cricket ground where a drumhead service was conducted at 3pm.

A special thanksgiving service took place at St. Peter's church at

Dismantling a defence post at the foot of Ditchling Rise, Brighton, in 1945.

11am the following day. Conducted by the Bishop of Lewes, the Right Reverend Hugh Horden, it was relayed to crowds outside.

Special bus services were laid on early on this day for the benefit of people travelling to places of worship. The special bus services operated from 10am to 1pm, when normal Sunday services were resumed.

Members of the Church of England in the Brighton rural deanery contributed the magnificent sum of £750 towards the purchase of a mobile canteen which was officially handed over to the Church Army on Wednesday 11th April 1945 at a presentation outside St Peter's church. This was preceded by a service of dedication conducted by Canon T. J. James, vicar of St. Anne's church, Kemp Town, and attended by the mayor and mayoress, Cr and Mrs A. V. Nicholls.

The canteen was destined for Germany, to provide refreshments for the Allied forces. (Brighton History Centre)

The Arrival of the First Bananas

The first consignment of bananas to arrive in Brighton since the beginning of the war arrived late on Monday night, 28th January 1946. Delivered to Elder and Fyffe's depot in New England Street, Brighton, they were kept in the warehouse until they ripened and were then sold in local greengrocer's shops around the town.

Imitation bananas hang tantalisingly in Mrs Speed's greengrocer's shop at no. 1 Sydney Street during the war years. (Mrs B. Tucknott)

The real thing at last! Was this child tasting his first ever banana which fell from a bunch during delivery in January, 1946, or is it a posed photograph? (Brighton History Centre)

Above: Roedean girls walking through the streets in Keswick, where the school was evacuated. HMS Vernon was based at the school during the war. (Daily Mail)

Below: The High Commissioner of Australia, Mr Bruce, with cadet officers from Australia at HMS King Alfred, Hove. (Brighton History Centre)

Home Guard, Military and Auxiliary Forces

Records for the 18th March 1943 indicate the following unit addresses in the local area. There were a large number of troops billeted in Brighton and Hove as well as the smaller adjacent towns. These military units were under strict orders to assist the civilian ARP and other rescue units in helping after air raid attacks and for that reason came under the local police units.

Unit	Base
10th Brighton Home Guard	22 Sussex Square, Brighton
11th Brighton Home Guard	Telephone House, Gloucester Place
14th Brighton Home Guard	51 Selborne Road, Hove
15th Brighton Home Guard	3 Dyke Road, Hove
'H' Company, 25th Brighton Sussex Home Guard	CME Works, Brighton Station
HMS Vernon	Roedean Girls School and St Dunstan's
HMS King Alfred	King Alfred Centre, Hove
RAF Station	Abbots Hotel, Brighton seafront
HM Coastguard Station	35 Adelaide Crescent, Hove
359th Coast Battery, R.A.	12 Chichester Terrace, Brighton
'A' Company ATS	Preston Barracks, Brighton
'E' Company ATS	Kings Hotel, Brighton
33rd Army Recruiting Centre	118 Queens Road, Brighton
National Fire Service	'Fairways', Dyke Road, Hove
ARP Controller (office)	47 Old Steine, Brighton
ARP Control Room	Devonian Court, Brighton
ARP Officer (office)	Circus Street, Brighton
ARP Officer & Controller	Court Farm Road, Hove

CANADIAN FORCES

During the summer of 1943 a large number of Canadian troops were posted to the Brighton/Hove area, being billeted in and around the two towns.

On the 23rd June 1943 the 2nd Canadian Corps were comfortably billeted in the Hove area. Brigadier John Smith of the 4th Canadian armoured division had his HQ in Wilbury Road, Hove. They were responsible for assistance in Hove in the event of an air attack, with a contact address at 23, Westbourne Villas, Hove.

Other units that had been posted to the area by 9th October 1943 included the following:

5th. Canadian Brigade with their HQ at 10 Grand Avenue, Hove

1st Battalion, The Black Watch (RHR) of Canada: HQ at 41, Fourth Avenue, Hove.

The 12th Light Field Ambulance: HQ at Hove College.

The Calgary Highlanders: Brigade HQ at Withdean Hall, Withdean Crescent, Brighton.

The visit of King George VI to the King Alfred, Hove. Here he inspects the Wrens at the training centre. (Brighton History Centre)

Hove's War Statistics

The following details have been extracted from official records.

CASUALTIES

Killed: 9 men, 12 women, 3 children and 6 servicemen. One man and a woman died subsequently as a result of their injuries. Total: 32
Seriously Injured: 14 men, 25 women, 1 child and 1 serviceman. Total: 41.
Slightly Injured: 39 men, 70 women and 15 children. Total: 124.
Total casualties: 190 civilians. 7 servicemen.

PROPERTY

Property totally destroyed by bombs, including those that were so badly damaged that they had to be demolished: 80.
Properties badly damaged: 134.
Properties with minor damage: 3,741
Properties sustaining very minor damage (broken windows or roof tiles): 1051.

AIR RAID WARNINGS (SIRENS):

Air raid warnings (red) from 3rd September 1939 until 2nd September, 1944: 1,059.
'Local pips' warnings (installed in June 1943): 194.

The largest number of 'red' air raid warnings in one day was eight, and this occurred on 27th October, 1940. The longest unbroken period of 'red' air raid warning sirens lasted from 6pm on 22nd November 1940 until 7.40am the following day, a total of 13 hours and 40 minutes.

ATTACKS

The two worst air attacks occurred in March 1943, during the 'tip and run' raids. These two raids resulted in a total of 104 casualties, including 22 deaths, and also caused very heavy damage to property in the town. There were also a number of lucky escapes during these years, none more than at the Shirley Street printing works, where 17 people were in the building when a bomb fell. Many of the workers were trapped and pinned by heavy machinery, but only eight of them suffered any injuries, including two who were seriously hurt.

Above: Part of Hove's sea defences.

Below: Nothing was needlessly discarded in wartime.

Death in a Room

On the evening of Wednesday 7th January 1942 several men from Portslade were detailed to undertake fire-watching duties at the premises of Holes and Davigdor Dairies in North Street, Portslade. Among them were Thomas Turnbull, the licensee of the Jolly Sailors public house, and William Rothwell, a labourer who worked on the roads.

The leader of this group of firewatchers, and the first one to report for duty at around 7pm, was William Chisholm of 76, Station Road in Portslade. He left the building a couple of times but returned around 9.45pm and spoke to one of the men who were leaving the premises. He later reported that he had spent a few minutes in the firewatcher's room. With the gas radiators on, the room had become very hot and so he had turned them off.

At about 10.15pm William Rothwell arrived, with Thomas Turnbull coming in a few minutes later. They booked on and then Turnbull left the premises for a few minutes. Chisholm left the building at around 10.50pm. Rothwell, left on his own, decided that he would light the radiators because he felt cold. Turnbull later returned, but at what time is unknown.

In the morning Mrs. Turnbull was anxiously waiting for her husband to return from his fire-watching duties, but at 8.20am he still hadn't come home. He usually arrived at about 7am, so she decided that she would go down to the premises to find him. It only took a few minutes for her to walk there. In the fire-watching room she could smell gas, and she found her husband sitting in a chair, dead.

She ran out, shouting for help. Across the road, outside his grocer's shop at 33, North Street, was Robert Bohanan. He rushed across the road and into the building and saw Turnbull dead in the chair. Smelling gas, he turned the radiators off straight away. He then saw Rothwell in a bed in the far corner of the room. He was fully dressed, apart from his boots and coat. He sent his son away to call the police, who arrived a few minutes later.

A doctor was called and he arrived at 9 o'clock. He examined the bodies and concluded that the two men had been dead for about five hours. At the inquest, held on 9th January, the doctor stated that in both cases death was due to coal gas poisoning and that in his opinion they died between 3am and 4am.

Rothwell's brother James, of 10, East Street, Portslade, identified his body. James Bates, a gas company technical supervisor, said that the radiator was in good working order and with no gas escapes. He later checked the gas radiator and it was agreed that it was unsuitable for a room with people sleeping in it.

The jury returned a verdict of accidental death on both men. The coroner extended his condolences to their families.

Another view of Hove's sea defences. Note the West Pier in the background. (Brighton History Centre)

A Wartime Police Reservist

This is the incredible story of a special constable in Hove during the war, Harry Clarke. Born in 1883, he was 5′ 6″ tall, married and living at 41a Cambridge Road. An employee of Hove Borough Council, he was also special constable no. 9.

In 1939, at the age of 56, he applied to become a full time police reservist, and after the usual checks effected by the chief officer of police he was accepted, becoming police war reserve constable No. 119. In 1941 he changed his address from Cambridge Road to no. 47 Lansdowne Street, paying a rent of a pound a week. At this time the estate agents Reason and Tickle wrote to the chief constable as to his suitability for being a tenant, a normal procedure in those days.

It wasn't long before Clarke had a complaint from a member of the public levelled against him. A Mr. Hutchinson of Lower Market Street reported an incident in the Western Hotel to the chief constable. Clarke had been at the bar and was engaged in general conversation. The subject later turned to permits, and at some stage Clarke had asked to see Hutchinson's. He knew that he had one because Hutchinson often boasted about it, but he had never seen one before. It was idle curiosity and he wanted to see what one looked like. It appears that Hutchinson showed his permit and then left the hotel.

A few days later they met up again, and Hutchinson demanded an apology for being embarrassed at the hotel by being made to produce his permit in public. Clarke refused to apologise and as a result the complaint was laid against him.

The chief constable found that Clarke had not usurped his powers, and a letter was written to Hutchinson informing him of this. The document in question was a curfew permit, which was necessary in order to move freely within the curfew zone. The incident arose chiefly because of a lack of training at that time. The war reserve policemen were taken on in a bit of a panic, as younger policemen were called away for military service.

Around this time the pay of war reserve policemen joining the service was £3 per week, with deductions taken for national health insurance, contributory pension and unemployment insurance. Part of the conditions of service was that there would be an 8-hour tour of duty. In the first year they might be required to attend training of not more than 20 hours, and in the second year a maximum of 12 hours. This training had to be undertaken in the officer's own time. There was some training in police time but the bookwork had to be done at home.

A few weeks after the unfortunate incident in the hotel Clarke was working a 2pm–10pm shift in Aldrington Basin at the Anglo American Depot. Because of his age, he didn't work the beat but was posted at various strategic premises as a police guard, keeping out unwanted visitors. It was a dark and bleak December night, with a cold wind blowing. He completed his shift at 10pm and began his journey home. There was no one about, and he thought of the warm fire and hot drink waiting for him when he got back. He was walking eastwards on the south side of the Basin. A wide jetty ran parallel

An incendiary bomb demonstration at the council yard in Leighton Road, Hove, in February, 1939. (Brighton History Centre)

with the road. Both the road and the jetty were made of identical materials, and there was no fence or wall at the water's edge.

Having lost his bearings, Harry Clarke missed his footing and fell into the icy water. There was a drop of about three feet, and the water was some nine feet deep. He shouted for help, but no one heard him. He continued to shout at the top of his voice, and after being in the water for ten minutes his cries were at last answered. By this time he was beginning to think that he would drown.

It was Percy Coleman, a switchboard operator for Brighton and Hove Gas Company, who heard him. He had left his workplace on the south side of the Basin when he heard shouts for help. He was unable to tell where they were coming from, and it was some five minutes before he saw the man in the water. With the aid of his torch he saw that Clarke was about three feet from the edge of the jetty. Just then another man, William Scarce, an able seaman from the *MV Ben Johnson* arrived with a boathook, and between them they got Clarke out of the water. He was just about all-in, and they gave him first aid.

Scarce, in his statement, said that he was sitting in the cabin when he heard shouts for help. He grabbed a torch and the boathook and hurried to where the man was in the water. Clarke was taken by ambulance to Hove Hospital. He returned to duty five days later. He had been wearing his police cape when he fell into the water, and it was recovered from the water the following day.

A few weeks later the police watch committee met and, after hearing the story from the chief constable, wrote to Coleman and Scarce thanking them for their 'splendid actions in the rescue of Clarke and which no doubt saved his life'. They awarded them the sum of two guineas (£2 2s) each.

On another occasion Clarke reported for night duty and was sent to the Leighton Road Corporation Depot, at this time the central control ARP post. His duty, as always, was to keep unauthorised people away from the property. During the night, at about 1.30am, he was visited by his sergeant, who found that 'all was correct'. The same sergeant visited him again at about 3.50am and was unable to find him. He searched the yard and the accessible buildings without success, and by now he was beginning to worry about his safety.

At about 4.35am Clarke emerged from a nearby building in the decontamination area. The sergeant told him that he had been looking for him for about 45 minutes and asked where he had been. Clarke replied that he had been walking about, to which the sergeant retorted that he had also been walking about – looking for him. The sergeant reported Clarke for 'neglect of duty,' and he later received a caution from the chief constable.

In May 1942 he was working at the Shell-Mex oil installation at Aldrington Basin. At about 12.15am the sergeant came to see him and found him fast asleep at his post. He faced a charge of 'neglect of duty' under the Temporary Constables Emergency Rules, section 4. He admitted the charge in front of the chief constable, and as a punishment he had his efficiency pay stopped for six months.

There were no further reports about Clarke, but he certainly had a rather exciting war.

Portslade on 8th April, 1942

Wednesday the 8th April was a peaceful spring like day and people were going about their business when without warning two Me. 109's, which had crossed the channel at wave height, suddenly attacked. Their target was the gasworks.

People dived for cover as soon as they realised what was happening, and the shore defences opened up. Both aircraft were carrying bombs slung under them, and they released them as they crossed the coastline: it is generally believed that the pilots just wanted to drop their bombs and get back across the channel quickly.

One bomb struck the no. 3 purifying shed and the Brighton, Hove and Worthing Gas Works in Aldrington Basin, Portslade. This severely damaged the plant, and part of the roof was blown away. The other bomb fell at the rear of the electricity works, just over the border in West Sussex.

At about 10.30pm on the same day a number of enemy aircraft machine-gunned and bombed Portslade and Southwick. The sirens had sounded their warnings before they arrived, and so people had time to take shelter. It was, nevertheless, a very frightening experience.

Serious damage was caused to residential premises and a number of people suffered injuries, some serious. Bombs also fell in the Fishersgate area during the raid.

An animal ambulance used locally during the 1940s.

Below: A National Fire Service booster pump in a pipeline on Hove seafront.

Portslade Gasworks

Thursday the 16th July 1942 was a lovely summer's day, with bright sunshine, very few clouds and the temperature in the high 70s. During the peace and tranquillity the residents of Portslade were suddenly jolted into life by a very large explosion – so loud that it was heard for miles around.

Soon, the National Fire Service was seen heading towards the Portslade Gasworks, where smoke was heading skywards. The fire was in the engine room and followed an explosion which had completely destroyed the roof of the building.

But for the prompt action by the NFS the fire could have been far more serious. Within half an hour of actually receiving the call, they had the outbreak under control.

The fire was caused, it was suspected, by a leak in a large gas main in the engine room that pumped foul gas into a purifier. The

The gasworks after the explosion.

room became gas-filled and a spark from an electric generator possibly ignited the gas.

One man, a gasworks employee, suffered a badly cut hand and was treated at the scene but refused to go to hospital, saying that he might go later.

The *Sussex Daily News* reported that Divisional Officer H. Stanislas was in charge of the fire-fighting arrangements. The roof was totally destroyed in the explosion while another close by was badly damaged by fire.

4th August, 1942

Tuesday 4th August, 1942 dawned a beautiful clear morning and very soon the sun was shining brightly. There were a few high clouds, which did tend to drop and cause the latter part of the morning to appear overcast, but these passed during the mid-afternoon.

At about 10.30am two Focke-Wulf 190s crossed the channel at wave height before ascending just prior to crossing the coastline at Southwick. The anti-aircraft guns in the coastal area immediately engaged them with intense fire, but they flew over the coast road heading northwards.

Shortly after crossing the coastline one of the enemy aircraft dropped its bomb, and then the two aircraft turned eastwards. The second bomb was then released and this struck houses in New Church Road near to the top of Berridale Avenue. It all but demolished two houses on the south side of Church Road when the bomb landed in the garden of no.108. An eyewitness later stated that he could see right through the houses as both the front and rear walls had collapsed. This bomb also caused blast damage over a wide area as well as injuring a number of people. One man was rushed to Hove hospital with severe injuries, having been rescued from his ruined home. The rescue services were soon engaged in a desperate digging operation to extricate a number of other people from would-be graves. A few hours later seven people had been pulled from the debris and taken to hospital – two men, four women and a child. Another 15 people, including four children, were also injured.

The other bomb had fallen in St. Richards Road, Southwick, and a large pall of smoke clearly indicated the exact spot. This bomb was responsible for the deaths of three of the six Southwick civilians killed during the war. Joyce Gatrell, a young mother aged 23 years, and her 21-month-old son, Roger, lived at no. 16, and the bomb scored a direct hit on their home, killing them instantly. Joyce was the wife of Corporal Charles Gatrell, who was serving with REME. Her parents lived at no. 55 Church Road, Portslade.

The third person to be killed was a 64-year-old factory worker, John Edwards, who lived at no. 1 Chapel Cottage, Fishersgate.

In the initial stages this did appear to be a 'nothing' incident as there were no indications of anyone injured or killed. Indeed, because of the intense noise from the anti-aircraft fire at the time of the raid many people were unaware that any bombs had fallen at all. In reality thirty people had suffered various types of injuries, three of them rushed to hospital for immediate treatment.

Among those who sustained injuries not deemed to be life threatening was a boy of three-and-a-half, Michael O'Shea. He had been sitting in his pushchair at his grandparents' house when the bomb fell, and he was extremely lucky to escape serious injury: he suffered two cuts to his head and a badly bruised forehead. His grandfather, Robert Browning, was not so lucky, as he suffered a broken leg.

Clouds of dust hampered the rescue services in the early stages. A YMCA tea waggon soon arrived, welcomed with a resounding cheer. Later another arrived, this time from the WVS.

St Richards Road, Southwick, where three people died, after the bombing raid in August, 1942.

Rodney Fuller's Story

After a letter in the local newspaper asking for information as part of the research for this book, I received a letter from Rodney Fuller. He related the following story, but freely admitted that he couldn't remember the actual date of the incident – he thought that it had possibly occurred around April, 1942, or the later part of the spring. As the months went by he gave me little snippets of information that helped to pinpoint the date. He then came across some letters at his home, addressed to his mother, and very soon, together with my own research, we were able to fix the date of this air attack as Tuesday 4th August 1942 – the raid covered in the previous chapter.

Mr Fuller now lives in Seaford, but in 1942 he was living at no. 97 New Church Road in Hove. I have left his story as he wrote it.

"I had spent the weekend at my grandfather's home in Worthing with my mother. He saw us onto a Southdown bus in Mill Road, Worthing, and we settled down for our journey home.

The bus trundled its well-run journey, all along the main A259 coast road where, along the Lancing stretch, some of the houses were made from old railway carriages. We then travelled over the old Norfolk Bridge and into Shoreham. I always made a point of looking at the pirate on the prow of his boat sticking out from the pub wall in Shoreham. We carried on over the humpy bridge where there were always two cranes hard at work, along past the lighthouse and then into Southwick.

There were not too many people on the bus, as we were travelling in mid-morning, in order to be home for lunch. I was sitting next to the window on the offside of the bus, and immediately we were in Southwick I had a very good view across the Basin towards 'Smokey Joe's' – that was our family's name for the electric power station's two large chimneys, which were always smoking.

What happened next, happened very quickly, but I remember it so vividly that it could have happened yesterday.

We saw two planes coming in across the sea straight towards the land. We thought that they must be the RAF, and a bit of a 'hooray' went up by the passengers. However, this stopped abruptly when the ack-ack opened up from their sites at the power station.

Someone shouted, 'They're Germans!' just as the bus was coming to its designated stop alongside a row of houses before reaching the Fishersgate Rec.

'Come along, we must all get off the bus,' was the general agreement, as the conductor led the passengers off. A scramble then ensued, but I was determined to watch what happened as long as possible, desperately wanting to stay and see it all.

The planes kept on coming towards us at speed and flew straight over the Basin. At the same time I saw something falling towards the land on our side of the Basin. Somewhere up ahead, but quite close by, was a very loud bang. By this time, though, we had been rushed into the first house that opened its doors, and everyone who could fit was pushed into a Morrison shelter in the front room. I don't think either the driver or conductor managed to get into the shelter, as I remember a lot of talking going on quite a distance above my head. We stayed in the shelter for what seemed a very long time, as it was starting to get very stuffy.

At last I heard a man say that it was now safe and we could get back on the bus. We got on and I ran to the front, as I wanted to see what had happened. The bus started, and we were off.

We came to what had been a little street on our left. The road in front of the bus was littered with broken bricks and other debris that had spilled down from the houses in the little street. There was a lot of broken glass, and it seemed to me that some of it was actually on fire. As the bus bumped its way over the bricks and other debris I looked up the street and saw smashed houses with lots of people pulling at the broken parts.

We were quickly past and the bus gathered a little speed as we went on down the hill and up again to the bottom of Boundary Road in Portslade. My mother said that we should get ready because our stop, at the bottom of Wish Road opposite the Lagoon, would soon be here.

We got off the bus at our stop and started to walk up Wish Road towards New Church Road. As we did so, I noticed that there were bits of broken tiles on the pavement. As we neared the top of the road we passed a man with a broom, who was sweeping the bits from his front pathway.

We reached New Church Road and turned right towards our house, and what a scene met our eyes! The whole road was full of people and especially outside our house. There were policemen, firemen and ARP wardens in their tin hats. There were nurses and various military personnel. They were centred on the two houses on the south side of New Church Road and opposite our house. They were scrambling over the remains of these houses, which were in a terrible state.

My mother then started to run and so did I. We came to a tape across the road and a policeman told us that we couldn't go any further. My mother said, 'That's my house over there and Nanny is in it.' We were then let through, and we rushed to the front door, which was open.

Nanny was all right, as when the sirens sounded she had quickly taken cover in the dining room that my grandfather had turned into a shelter by blocking the windows and then using scaffolding poles and thick planks of wood to prop up the ceiling in order that it wouldn't collapse.

I had a quick look downstairs and found that we had no windows left and that the ceiling had come down in the lounge. I went upstairs and that was just the same, with windows broken and the ceilings down. Incredibly though, the roof tiles seemed to be intact. The other damage I saw was that the garage doors had been blown off.

The bomb had landed in the rear garden of no. 108 New Church Road, causing massive blast damage.

I spent as long as I was able looking out of the front window and watching the scene opposite in total awe. The rescue services were working flat out. I was fascinated by the fact that I could see right through the houses, as they had lost both the front and back walls. I wasn't allowed to stay very long as my mother soon hurried me away.

We left the house that day as it had to be boarded up to await its turn to be repaired and we went over the downs to spend the rest of the war in Hassocks."

Additional note by Rodney Fuller:
"I believe the first bomb in Portslade fell in the vicinity of Mill Road
or in Brambledean. This area has been redeveloped and it is difficult
to be certain.

In St.Richard's Road it appears that all the original property is still
standing. There is still a building on the south side of the A259 that
I remember as being there at the time of this bomb falling and would
be almost opposite the end of the bombed street."

27th July, 1942

Monday 27th July 1942 started very bright and sunny, with a slight breeze coming in from the channel – a wonderful day for residents of Hove. It had been more than a year since the last air attack on the town and many of them believed that for them the wartime bombs had finished, although the town did have quite a large population of military personnel and might therefore be targeted.

Local people constantly read about the bombing of other cities and towns and their thoughts turned to sympathy, especially when the newspapers reported the deaths of children. During the past month Brighton had suffered three bombing raids, although fortunately no one had been killed.

At about 6.40 am the sirens sounded their warning and the few people then on the streets hurried to the nearest shelters. A German bomber was seen, and although the coastal defences opened up in an

Sandbags surround a warden's post in Wilbury Villas, at the junction with the Upper Drive, Hove. (Brighton History Centre)

effort to destroy the incoming raider, it dropped four high explosive bombs and escaped without any visible damage.

It was generally believed that the coastal guns had frightened off the raider, because the bombs fell harmlessly in the sea about a hundred feet south of the Adur hotel, just east of the harbour. Huge spouts of water rose high in the air as the bombs exploded, but no damage was caused to any of the seafront properties.

Site unknown. This bombed house was in Hove, but no more precise location has been discovered.

9th August, 1942

This was one of the worst raids to date as several enemy planes were heard over the town. It was almost 11pm on Sunday, 9th August when the first activity was heard. The sounds of the sirens had already died away when the drone of enemy aircraft were heard.

The residents, safe in their shelters, braced themselves and waited for the sounds of the falling bombs. The vast majority of the 21 high explosive bombs fell on the West Hove area, with a number of residential homes suffering severe damage, and they were accompanied by nearly a thousand incendiary bombs that caused numerous small fires in about 50 homes.

Once again no serious damage resulted in these fires but it kept the residents occupied for a while. There were no fatal casualties, although a number of people suffered serious injuries. Four men and seven women, two of them elderly, eventually recovered in hospital.

The rescue workers spent the rest of the night at the various scenes, not only helping the injured people but clearing up the debris.

Two of the bombs fell in Benfield Crescent, seriously damaging a convent and a number of residential houses. One woman was rescued from the wreckage of her home after about two hours and was given first aid before she was taken to the Hove Hospital.

Two other bombs struck houses and business properties in Foredown Drive, causing extensive damage and injuring three people including a young child. After treatment in hospital, they returned to their relatives' homes to be looked after because their own were too badly damaged.

One bomb dropped on a school playground, scoring a direct hit on the entrance to an air raid shelter. This resulted in considerable blast damage to surrounding properties.

The safety afforded by Morrison shelters undoubtedly saved several lives. At one point a high explosive bomb crashed into the roadway, causing severe damage to the houses with debris being scattered over a wide area. When the rescuers penetrated the huge pile of debris they found two occupants in the shelter unhurt, although somewhat unnerved. Another man further down the street was also rescued from his shelter. When asked if he was all right, he said, 'Yes, I'm all right, but look at my bloody house!'

A keen gardener swore vengeance against Hitler when he found that an incendiary bomb had burnt itself out in his garden, but not before it had destroyed a large portion of his crop of runner beans.

The roof and part of the stand at the Brighton and Hove football ground was also damaged in this raid. Two houses were completely wrecked, while a number of others sustained severe damage.

One of the bombs had damaged a water main at one location and the road started to flood. There had been a lengthy dry spell and water at that time was very precious, so more men from the water works were called upon to assist with the repairs.

Another of the bombs fell and exploded in Hove Cemetery, dislodging many gravestones. It was a major job to replace them accurately and to put the cemetery back to rights. Many people, especially women, were very upset when they saw the damage to the graves of their loved ones, roundly cursing the Germans and their bombs.

Bomb damage to houses in Park Lane, Southwick.

24th August, 1942

Monday morning, 24th August 1942 started gloriously. On the outskirts of the town the heat haze glistened. The sea was a wonderful bright blue, and although it was wartime, people were relaxed and happy.

By late afternoon one or two clouds started to drift across the sky, and at 5.55pm the whole town was put on alert as the sirens sounded their alarm. Many residents who were just starting their evening meal quickly made their way to their shelters, some children clutching their sandwiches as they were hurried along.

A single enemy aircraft seen flying lying low over the town strafed the western end of Hove and the eastern end of Portslade with machine gun and canon fire, injuring two people. A single bomb was dropped, crashing on no. 21 Station Road, Portslade, and causing severe damage. It ricocheted through a wall into an adjoining building, then through the front of the building and up and over the rooftops before landing in Worcester Villas. It

Bomb damage in Worcester Villas.

exploded in the garden of an adjoining residential property. This caused very serious damage with several residents being buried beneath the debris of their homes.

Serious damage was also caused to a dance academy, one of the two houses where the bomb exploded. Fourteen children trapped in a shelter beneath the stairs were rescued by police and ARP Rescue workers. The children were very lucky and were only suffering from shock, cuts and bruises although the house was almost demolished.

A wardrobe upstairs was left intact on the merest remnant of a floor, while another wardrobe a short distance away was only slightly damaged. Blast damage was caused over a wide area with many properties suffering severe damage including many of those in Boundary Road. Machine gun fire raked properties previously damaged and close to obtaining their final repairs.

Yet again, the rescue services were quickly on the scene, being applauded for their promptness by the local council at their next meeting. The various civil defence departments were now attuned to the art of rescue work and quickly got organised soon after their arrival at the scene. Their labours continued very late into the night, a middle aged woman being the last to be rescued, just before 10.30pm. She was rushed to hospital with serious injuries.

The police had cordoned off the road within minutes of the bomb exploding, allowing only the emergency services through the rope

Children were rescued from under the stairs at the dance academy in Worcester Villas.

barriers, but many sightseers gathered to view the damage as soon as the 'All Clear' had sounded, their evening meal well forgotten. They stood quietly watching the various aspects of the rescue work going on and making way for the small ambulances to leave, taking the injured to the hospital in Hove.

At the final count of the casualties, those seriously injured were four men and two women. Those injured and needing hospital treatment numbered eight men, four women and two children. Twelve people were treated at the scene for minor injuries – mainly facial cuts caused by flying glass.

12th October, 1942

About 12.25pm on Monday 12th October 1942 a determined attack on Brighton around the railway station and the Seven Dials area resulted in properties just across the border into Hove being damaged, too. Large 500kg bombs were dropped.

The roads where blast damage occurred included Goldsmid Road, Addison Road, Dyke Road and Melville Road. A number of properties in Brunswick Terrace suffered external damage due to machine gun and canon fire from the attacking German aircraft.

The damage was referred to as 'slight' in the official documents. There was one minor casualty – a young girl who suffered a small cut to the head when she was struck by a piece of flying glass. Two elderly women were comforted after suffering shock.

Two civil defence rescue squads attended the area, but apart from the small amount of clearing up and attending to the young girl's cut there was little else to do. They were dispatched with other units from Hove to assist the Brighton rescue squads.

A Machine Gun Attack

On the 27th November 1942 a new and very unpopular undertaking was added to the German pilot's routine. Following a verbal 'Fuhrerbefehl' (Hitler order) conventional fighter units of the Luftwaffe were now to begin 'Terrorangriffe' – terror attacks on southern England. The orders were to attack and strafe purely civilian targets, which in particular meant those people unlucky enough to be caught out in the streets. One of the first of these types of attacks involved Hove – a mere three days later on the 30th November.

At 12.25pm two Focker Wulf 190s flying low across the Channel approached the town in 'line of flight' from the south-east. They were seen as they approached and quickly lost height as they attacked. People ran for their lives, picking up their children as they went and finding whatever shelter they could.

This was certainly a terror attack, the likes of which had not been seen before. The residents of the area were terrified as hundreds of machine gun bullets and canon shells rained down. Later they said they expected to hear the sounds of bombs falling after the attack, not only the guns.

One woman who had been in her garden but had managed to run indoors said that she had never been so frightened, and that the noise was deafening. Another woman said that she had just returned from shopping and saw a German plane flying low straight down her street, firing its guns. The noise was horrible, and she didn't have time to get her key out to open her front door, simply flattening herself against the door in desperation.

It had been about six weeks since any action had been experienced, and this had caught people totally unprepared. The German attackers were certainly achieving their aim. Bullets could be heard ricocheting off the many buildings that were hit.

The town at this lunchtime was systematically fired upon. Some of the worst damage was caused to residential properties in Godwin Road and Bellingham Crescent. Loud screams were heard from one property as a bullet went through a window, narrowly missing the two children inside. They were uninjured, but their mother was treated for shock.

A street lamp in Godwin Road, about 300ft from the junction of Bellingham Crescent, was struck by cannon fire which knocked the top part to the ground. It was found in the road some yards away.

The general feeling by townsfolk at the time was that it was a deliberate attack on the children who were making their way home from the local school, which was approximately 200 yards south-east from the damaged houses. It was certainly a near miracle that there were no fatalities among the children. Two of them fell and cut themselves while trying to reach some shelter, and they were given first aid in their own homes.

This was a typical 'tip and run' raid as the attack was quickly over, both aircraft roaring out to sea across the western part of Hove.

Once the raiding aircraft had gone people came streaming out of their homes to see what had happened. Excited neighbours talking about the attack soon filled Godwin Road. The general feeling was that they had all been lucky: no bombs was a godsend. Somebody found a cannon cartridge and very soon the children were out searching for souvenirs. Several more cartridge cases were found as well as two aluminium fuses and six links of belt used with cannon shells.

One small boy, very excited, announced that he was keeping a cartridge case he had found in a shoebox along with a piece of shrapnel he had discovered after an earlier raid.

The *Brighton & Hove Herald* of 5th December, 1942 reported, 'A cannon fire attack was made by two low flying enemy planes on a housing estate on the outskirts of a south coast town on Monday. There were no casualties and only slight damage was reported.'

Hove – 1943

The following are details for the Hove area for 1943 obtained from the East Sussex Record Office.

Portslade
January 30th 1943
At 15.25 hours a German mine was washed up due to the rough seas and exploded causing slight damage to properties in the vicinity of the seafront. There were no injuries reported.

Hove
January 31st
A coastal defence sea-mine exploded at 04.45 hours opposite the eastern end of Portslade Gasworks. Severe damage was caused to a number of Army huts situated on the seafront. Lesser damage was

A Morrison shelter in the ruins of no. 5 Shelley Road, Hove, after an air attack on 9th March, 1943. (Author's collection)

caused to a number of other properties in the area. There was no serious damage reported to the gasworks complex.

March 9th
Four German aircraft [FW 190s] attacked Hove. The red warning was timed at 16.53 hours. The bombs started to fall approximately one minute after the alert.

At 18.18 hours Hove controller reported to HQ as follows: '2 dead, 25 casualties detained in Hove hospital.' The report continued, '3 persons trapped in Shelly Road, some in Carlisle Road and some in Rutland Gardens. We might need the detector van and some rescue parties.'

At 19.14 hours the following were organised and despatched: 2 ambulances and 3 casualty cars were sent from Portslade. This was as well as another 4 ambulances, 2 casualty sitting case cars, two first aid parties and a YMCA canteen van.

Reports indicated that the railway line near Aldrington Halt had been damaged by one of the bombs. The 'up' line about 50 yards west of the station had suffered some damage and this was quickly repaired and the line was reopened soon after 8pm.

Later reports indicated that there was damage to properties in Shelley Road, Aldrington Gardens, Carlisle Road, Rutland Gardens and Modena Road. A rest centre was opened at the Portland Road School. There were 6 dead. One man, a painter, was missing and 30 persons were detained in hospital.

May 18th
The newly installed local air raid alarm system was first tested on Sunday 16th May and was then tested daily at 10am.

May 25th
The first report of 'bombs and gunfire' was timed at 12.26pm. One of the first reports received by the controller was that the gasholder in Church Road was on fire having been struck by German FW 190s. The National Fire Service managed to extinguish the flames at 13.33 hrs having obtained assistance from Portslade and Shoreham appliances.

Minor damage was caused to properties in the vicinity of Church Road by canon and machine gun fire. One male person suffered gunshot wounds and was taken to Hove hospital.

Although Hove had been attacked, this was minor compared to Brighton and several rescue parties were sent to Brighton where more than 20 HE bombs had been dropped and there being classed a 'major' incident. The rescue squads and first aid parties had returned to their various depots by 19.45 hours.

June 26th
09.45 hours – reported that the gasholder in Church Road had still not been repaired and this was causing serious disruption to people living in the area.

August 11th
20.20 hours – report of a petrol tank jettisoned from a Spitfire and landed in the garden of 33, Elm Drive. Incident timed at 19.05 hours.

September 11th
It was reported that the repairs being carried out on the gasholder in Church Road were still not completed.

November 22nd
Gasholder in Church Road was still being repaired and there were hopes that they would be completed by the end of the year.

December 9th
The Regional ARP Services ran a night exercise to test out the local ARP sections in getting quickly to 'call out' incidents.

At 20.45 hours a message was sent to the units at Hove and Portslade and put them on 'standby' to assist an imaginary incident at Worthing. All units at these stations were poised to turn out quickly, believing that the 'call out' would come almost straight away after the 'standby', as several of these exercises had in the past. They were just beginning to relax when the call out came at 21.10 hours.

The 'call' was to Portslade for one ARP rescue party and to Hove for one rescue party and one ambulance. The rendezvous was given as the Downlands Hotel, Upper Brighton Road, followed by the map reference number of 585.243. The rescue party left Portslade at 21.43 hours and the Hove unit at 21.02 hours. They attended the rendezvous and after a short briefing and discussion left for their home bases. The Portslade party who only had 5 members instead of the usual 6 left the Rendezvous at 23.30 hours arriving back soon after midnight. The senior controller at the regional HQ who had organised the exercise wanted to know at length why there were only the 5 members of the team and it was reported that one was on holiday while the other was sick.

The Hove rescue party and the ambulance left Worthing at 21.55 hours. The rescue party arrived back at their Hove base at 1am while the ambulance arrived five minutes later. However, at 00.45 hours the regional HQ contacted the Hove controller as follows: 'We want to know what units Hove sent, as there seems to be some difference in the reports they have received at Worthing.' Hove reported that they sent one rescue unit with 7 men and the ambulance with driver only.

Note

While all this was going on the military were also conducting exercises and had been using flares on the downs between Telscombe and Kingston. There was also a 'special services' night operation being carried out at the Birling Gap area between 8pm and 1am. These involved parachutists being dropped and landings made. Spotlights and red lamps were used. Was this an exercise in preparation for D-Day?

December 15th

Several reports of a damaged water main at Kingston Buci, spilling gallons of water. One unit NFS sent at 22.15 hours. The following day it was reported that the water main had been repaired and in answer to a question posed by the regional controller, it was reported the gasholder in Church Road had still not been repaired to working order.

Note

A report in respect of the gasholder in Church Road indicated that it was finally repaired and working correctly on 12th May 1944.

Sea-mines off Hove and Portslade

New Year of 1943 was very bleak, but as 1942 had been a quite a calm year for the local residents there was at least something to try to be positive about. Meanwhile the weather could only be described as awful. There were very low temperatures, severe frost and snow, and as January progressed there were the problems of severe gales.

Throughout the year there were a number of vast explosions causing damage along the Brighton, Hove and Portslade seafronts.

January 30th 1943, Portslade – At 3.25pm on Saturday a German mine was washed up due to the rough seas and exploded, causing slight damage to properties in the vicinity of the seafront. There were no casualties.

January 31st 1943, Hove – A coastal defence mine exploded at 4.45am on Sunday opposite the East End of Portslade Gasworks. This caused severe damage to a number of army huts situated on the seafront. Lesser damage was caused to residential properties in the area. There was no serious damage caused to the gasworks complex. No civilian personnel were injured.

March 9th 1943, Hove – At 2.10pm on Tuesday a sea mine exploded opposite Adelaide Crescent, causing extensive damage to windows in residential properties along the seafront.

December 16th 1943, Hove – At 3.09pm on Thursday there was a report of a coastal defence mine exploding at Kingsway. It was later reported that a Canadian Army sergeant was killed while trying to defuse the mine and make it safe. The damage caused by the explosion was confined to a number of residential properties having their windows broken.

Above: Shelley Road, Hove, struck by a bomb on 9th March, 1943. The bomb, dropped at low level, went through the roof of premises in Portland Road before hitting nos. 1 and 3. (Author's collection)

Below: Women salvage their belongings from their homes in Shelley Road. (Brighton and Hove Herald)

9th March, 1943

Shortly before 5 o'clock on the very pleasant spring afternoon of Tuesday 9th March, 1943, the air raid sirens sounded the warning of an attack. On this occasion local residents had just about enough time to hurry to their shelters. Shortly after the sirens started the 'pips' were heard, indicating that enemy aircraft were close. Witnesses heard the distinctive engine sounds of German aircraft as four Focker Wulf 190s launched their attack. They came in very low, one just missing the spire of a church in the southern part of the town. They came in from the southeast in two's, line abreast, each of them carrying a 500kg bomb. The pilots waited until the very last moment before releasing their deadly cargo, first softening up the town with canon and machine gun fire.

One aircraft singled out Aldrington railway station, and its bomb scored a hit on the railway lines about 50 yards west of the station. The blast from this bomb damaged the railway station and put the 'up' line out of action for about five hours: it was repaired and opened just after 10pm, when normal service was resumed. Although Aldrington Halt railway station suffered some blast damage, the station was still kept in service.

One of the other bombs was dropped from the southern side of the town and took on the guise of a torpedo as it descended through the air. This bomb crashed through the roof space of a shop with living quarters above in Portland Road, causing roof tiles and wooden rafters to land in adjacent streets. It then crossed Portland Road before burying itself and exploding on no. 3, Shelley Road. Another bomb fell and exploded in Rutland Gardens, while the fourth struck houses in Walsingham Terrace. All these bombs caused death, destruction and heartache.

The 'red' alert warning was timed at 4.53pm and the bombs began to fall one minute later. People in the streets ran for cover as the bullets and canon fire rained down.

Fred Hodgkinson had left his home at no. 18, Jesmond Road to visit his sick daughter in Aldrington Avenue. He was about to run for cover when a bullet struck him. A man ran to his assistance but it was too late to help him.

The local newspapers reported this incident in detail. Hodgkinson was a well-known local journalist who had retired several years before. For a number of years he had been a sub editor for the *Sussex Daily News,* and at one time he was editor of the *Evening Argus.* He later became staff correspondent in Brighton for the *Evening Standard,* a job that had transformed a quietly efficient local journalist into one of the best-known and respected reporters of his day.

For many years he lived in Abbey Road, Brighton, and was often seen strolling along the seafront in the Kemp Town area, a very friendly and likable man. He was a chorister at St. Anne's Church in Burlington Street.

His daughter Mollie was the wife of Pc Lionel Piper, and they had a 7-year-old son, David. She used to work as an assistant at Beal's bookshop in East Street, Brighton, but she was seriously ill at this time and the death of her father is believed to have hastened her death. She was taken to hospital five days later on Sunday 14th March and died the following Thursday.

Just before the bomb struck at the homes in Shelley Road, young Dinah Heward was sent out across the road to call her sister in. (See the following chapter.) She and some friends were talking to Mr Thomas of no. 3, Shelley Road, who was in the process of painting the outside of his house. As the sirens sounded he invited the children in to shelter but they refused and hurried back across the road to their own home. A minute later the bomb struck the house and he was killed: those children had been very lucky.

Rescue services were soon on the scene, aided by military personnel, many of whom were Canadian soldiers stationed in the town, while another group of rescue workers tackled the badly damaged houses in Rutland Gardens where the body of 81-year-old Elizabeth Bouchier was recovered from the ruins of her home as the daylight faded.

Several local council workers were injured when bomb blast and machine-gun bullets damaged their depot nearby.

Meanwhile Enid Smith and her friend Gwen Dawes (née

Rutherford) had left Brighton railway station by train. Their destination was Aldrington Halt, and they arrived just as the raid was starting. They had just left the station when the German plane began to machine-gun the streets. Running for their lives, they just about made it to the tunnel under the track. This afforded them some shelter, but they caught the blast from the bomb that hit the railway track and it blew them off their feet. They suffered no real injury, however, and emerged rather ruefully from their shelter on their way home.

It was the blast from this bomb that demolished the house in Amhurst Crescent and badly damaged a number of adjoining properties. Harold Sparks who lived at no. 6 with his wife was badly injured. She had quite a remarkable escape. She was in the next room when the bomb exploded, and managed to crawl out from the debris suffering shock and a few cuts and scratches. Her husband was later extricated from the debris, seriously injured, and he died in Hove hospital the following day.

A little way away one of the bombs hit a row of houses in Walsingham Terrace, a road off the seafront. This bomb reduced two houses to a very large pile of rubble. The bomb exploded on no. 10, and six people lost their lives, all at this one address.

All the witnesses mentioned a strange quietness immediately after the explosion. In the eerie silence, even the traffic noises seemed hushed. Then there were sounds in abundance – screams and cries for help, followed by shouts of, 'We're coming!' and the footsteps of many people running to help the victims. In a short while the rescue and first aid parties were arriving, dismantling the pile of rubble with bare hands.

Mrs Edith Wakerly was 30 years old in March 1943 and married to George Wakerly, a gunner with the Royal Artillery. They had a son, Michael who was five years old and attended the local school. They lived at no. 10c, Walsingham Terrace – a large house divided into flats. On Tuesday 9th March 1943 Gunner Wakerly was home on a few days leave and the family were enjoying this short time together. They had been out for the best part of the day but had returned in time for their evening meal. The weather had stayed fine all day, but now a slight sea mist was coming in from off the sea. Young Michael had already told his mother that he was hungry and had asked several times what he was being given for his meal.

Just before 5 o'clock the dreaded sirens sounded their mournful wail and the Wakerlys quickly made their way to a 'walk in' cupboard under the stairs that was used as a shelter and believed to be the safest place in the house. The meal would have to wait.

In the house with them at this time was Mrs Wakerly's 56-year-old widowed mother, Florence Priest: she was living with her daughter for the duration of the war. She also went to shelter in the cupboard with her daughter and grandson, but George Wakerly was still making his way there when the bomb fell.

They would have heard the German Focke-Wulf aircraft overhead but they probably never heard the bomb that killed them. Clouds of dust and dirt indicated the precise location of where it had fallen – a direct hit. The rescue services were quickly on the scene, helped by dozens of Canadian soldiers. Several lorries stood by to remove the mountain of debris that, a very short while before, had been a house.

As darkness fell another rescue unit was brought in to relieve the initial team, and work continued well into the night until they heard a moaning noise. Their efforts took on a new intensity, and soon they found George Wakerly, who was severely injured. He was rushed to Hove hospital, where he would spend many months being treated for his wounds. Soon afterwards the bodies of Miss Gertie Knight and Mrs Alexandra Lea, both aged 51 years, were found. The work now continued with the aid of shaded lamps and torches.

During the following morning the rescuers reached the bodies of Mrs. Wakerly and her little boy, huddled together. They had been badly injured and had died together, while the body of Mrs Priest was soon found nearby.

Rescue parties were desperately moving the rubble in Rutland Gardens after one of the rescuers stated that he heard a faint cry coming from beneath the ruins of the house.

At 6.18pm the Hove controller reported to his HQ as follows: 'Two dead and 25 casualties detained in Hove hospital.' The report continued, 'Three persons trapped in the debris of their homes in

Rescuing personal belongings from a house in Rutland Gardens after the raid of 9th March, 1943.

Shelley Road while others were trapped in Carlisle Road and Rutland Gardens. We might need the detector van and more rescue parties.' A unit was requested to some houses in Medina Road where damage had occurred.

Within a few minutes the ARP Controller had sufficient information to organise the rescue. It was about 7.15pm when he requested assistance from Portslade and Brighton as a matter of urgency. Portslade sent two ambulances and three casualty cars while another four ambulances, two sitting case cars and two first aid parties were despatched from Brighton. The controller also requested a canteen refreshment vehicle to be sent to the area as it was obvious that the rescue would go on well into the night. These canteen vehicles were often in attendance at rescue scenes. Another one was sent from Burgess Hill.

It wasn't very long before more and more rescue units appeared on the scene and once again more refreshment vehicles were requested. Within an hour or so two such vehicles arrived on the scene. One being supplied by the YMCA and another supplied by the WVS. A third vehicle turned up shortly after these. supplied by the Salvation Army. Throughout the war years these three units did sterling and admirable work at all rescue scenes.

The controller then requested yet another rescue unit, this being supplied from Portslade. The casualty lists were growing and Hove hospital in Sackville road reported that almost 30 people had been admitted, suffering from a variety of injuries. A rest centre was opened at the Portland Road School.

Early indications were that five people had been killed, but several more had not been accounted for. The rescue units toiled away, and they were still working at the scene at midnight. Another refreshment vehicle had been requested, and that arrived from Brighton just after 11pm.

The digging and removal of the debris continued well into the night at all the devastated sites. One or two people were pulled from the wreckage of their homes, badly injured but alive.

A few days later, and after several hours of negotiation, Hove Council agreed to pay all costs relating to the food and drink supplied by the refreshment vehicles from 16.54 hours on the 9th for a period of 48 hours. This indicates that the rescue work continued for far longer than is officially recorded.

The final casualty totals were 12 people killed, 30 seriously injured and 21 suffering with a degree of slight injuries: some of these needed hospital treatment but were not detained.

One of the most dramatic experiences of this air attack was that of Mrs. Wood. She lived in the flat above her shop in Portland Road. She was in her bedroom with her daughter when she saw a German plane coming straight towards her windows as if about to fire into the room. The plane released a bomb that she thought had bounced off the roof of her home before falling on houses in Shelley Road, where it exploded. The first realisation that the bomb had struck her house was a crash and the fall of plaster from the ceiling, revealing a hole in the roof – the bomb had passed between the roof rafters. Three houses in Shelley Road were almost completely demolished, and the houses opposite suffered severe blast damage.

Members of the National Air Raid Precautions animal committee were kept very busy at this incident. Among the many animals rescued was a batch of 40 rabbits, which had been buried when a garage collapsed on the hutches: all but one were recovered alive.

An article in the *Sussex Daily News* of 11th March, 1943, reported that 'Two neighbouring girls' school hockey teams were involved in a match when the German raiders passed overhead. One of the team players said, "The sirens went but there didn't seem to be anything on and so we continued to play." When the plane came over a number of the girls lay down flat and the teachers called for the others to do the same. You could see bullets leaving the plane. They were silver tracer bullets and afterwards a few cases were found on the field.

Some of the girls subsequently made for the school buildings and others for the hedge, beneath which they crawled towards the school. The goalkeeper lay down in the goal and a metal, bronze coloured case fell by her, causing a 'weal' in the ground. The referee ran the whole length of the field while bullets were flying around.'

When the 'raiders passed' sounded the two teams continued their game, but shortly afterwards the 'Alert' sounded again and this time the match was abandoned.

A few days later the media's interest was alerted when they found that one of the victims was a former Scotland Yard police officer, 82-year-old Thomas Divall, who lived with his housekeeper, Edith Besant, at no. 1, Shelley Road. Chief Inspector Divall was thought to have been involved in the investigations into the 'Jack the Ripper' murders in Whitechapel, London, at the turn of the century.

This raid coincided with one at Worthing about the same time when a large number of people were killed. The following day German radio announced that 'Fast German bombers made a surprise daylight raid on Worthing yesterday bombing public utility plants and other military installations.' In a later broadcast, it was stated that 'in a low level attack; the western part of Worthing was particularly hard hit, whole blocks of buildings collapsed.'

There was, however, no mention of Hove.

Diana Heward's Story

"In March 1943 I was six years old and living at no. 20, Shelly Road in Hove. My sister was seven, and my brother was just a year old.

At around teatime on Tuesday 9th March the air raid sirens started their familiar wail, indicating an air attack by German aircraft. My parents struggled to release my young brother from his pram harness. I was sent out into the street to call my sister in. I ran over to no 3, where she was talking to our friends and to our friend's father, Mr. Thomas. As the sirens had already sounded Mr Thomas invited us all to shelter in his house until the 'all clear' sounded. We refused his offer and hurried back across the road to our home.

We were so fortunate, because moments later his house received a direct hit from a bomb. We had run indoors and had just got into our Morrison shelter when the brown taped windows blew in, momentarily hanging in space before they dropped.

It is a little strange at this point, as we were not supervised in the shelter and my sister and I must have run out a split second after the bomb had exploded. We saw the houses that had just been hit suspended in the air. The masonry somehow separated and then it dropped back into a dusty heat haze. My father in later years confirmed this, and I think he must have come along the hallway and sent us back into the shelter. This obviously happened in a split second – it was very weird.

At this time we were at the back of the house and the blast came not from the bomb in Shelley Road but from the one that exploded in Rutland Gardens. All hell broke loose, the air filling with just about every sound you could imagine. Moments later the bomb landed in Shelley Road and exploded with a tremendous noise. This bomb had not fallen straight down but had acted a little similar to a torpedo and passed through the roof of a greengrocer's shop in Portland Road and then across the road before exploding on the house in Shelley Road.

We were led out of the house by rescuers and I remember walking over the front door, as it was off its hinges and on the floor. There was glass, dirt and dust everywhere. I can still see the great pall of grey dust that hung in a sort of cloud in the gap between the remaining houses. It was an incredible sight: nos. 1, 3 and 5 no longer existed and no. 7 was so badly damaged that it had to be demolished. I remember being told that a boy older than me and his grandmother had to be rescued from their shelter in one of the houses.

My father, William Salisbury, was 44 years old at this time and had failed his medical to join the services during the First World War. He was found to have a heart condition. He served an apprenticeship with Daimlers, building war vehicles at their factory in London. In 1926 he moved to Hove, and became the proprietor of the West Hove Sheet Metal Works – a reserved occupation, of course. I remember that he worked endless hours on war production, sub-contracted to C.V.A. in Portland Road, and I also think to Hounslow's, in Portslade.

At around teatime on the 9th March he was returning from delivering some finished war work to one of these companies. He called in home on the way back to his company in Goldstone Street. My mother gave him a letter from my aunt to read and also made him a cup of tea. Needless to say, he didn't read the letter – in fact he *never* did, as the letter disappeared and we never did find it. However, this letter saved his life, as he would have been getting into his car outside had he not stopped for that short time. The car survived the blast but was quite badly damaged. It received another blast later in the month in Goldstone Street, where my father was when the Shirley Press was bombed.

Sadly, our friend's father Mr. Thomas, who we had been talking to moments before the bomb fell, was killed along with his next-door neighbours. He had been painting his house while he was on leave from the army, I think. Immediately after the bomb exploded the rescuers found the ladder he had been using smashed and blown apart, the bits scattered over the roadway. The immediate thought was that he, too, had been blown apart, but my mother informed the rescuers that she had spoken to my sister and me, and that we had told her that he was going indoors when the sirens sounded. My mother also told them that he had a 'blast wall' outside the dining room window. During the rescue they dug their way through the rubble in the area of the dining room and eventually found his body on a mattress there, under a pile of debris.

The rescuers arrived very promptly, but the first people on the scene were Miss Kibblewhite and Mrs. Cooper. Mrs Cooper lived just up the Street, at no. 34 and Miss Kibblewhite, my headmistress, was visiting her. They both taught at Aldrington School in Portland Road.

We were taken with our friends to no. 34, Shelley Road, for shelter. When we came out of the house a lot of people had arrived – wardens and troops who were stationed in the area.

The damage in Shelley Street was severe at the lower end, and the damage existed right up to about no. 24 on one side and no.15 on the other. To this day I can still see the difference in the brickwork where new ones replaced those blown out in the bombing. The roofs were very badly damaged. New front doors were required up to no. 26 on the west side. Several lamp-posts were blown out of the ground and were lying haphazardly across the road

I remember falling asleep in our house that night, listening to the water tank giving a constant drip, drip, drip. The next morning the sun shone brightly through the holed roof, my mother remarking that at first she thought she had left the light on all night.

By this time the wardens had erected a rope barrier at each end of the road, allowing only workmen and residents in. The bombed houses opposite were just a very large pile of debris with rescuers frantically searching for the people buried underneath. One other thing that sticks in my mind is a soldier adjusting his hat in the remains of my mother's dressing table mirror. The curtains had twisted so tightly and the furniture was splintered with glass.

We were very lucky, as we suffered no serious injuries, although my father did have a number of cuts, mainly to the forehead, from the broken windows at the back of our house. The occupier of no. 8 was in Brighton at the time of the bombing. The house was badly damaged, and she collapsed with shock when she arrived home."

STORIES FROM THE MEDIA

Many interesting stories can be found in the local wartime newspapers. Here are two that I found in the *Brighton and Hove Herald* on the 20th March 1943. I believe that both relate to the raid on Hove on 9th March when many streets were machine-gunned.

'After taking shelter during a recent South Coast 'sneak raid', a woman returned to her kitchen to find the window broken and water hissing from a pipe.

A cannon shell had been fired through the kitchen window and had set fire to the curtains. The shell had then struck a cold-water pipe, causing it to throw out a jet of water, which then put out the fire.'

'Domestic pets are not forgotten when air raids occur. As an instance of this, we are reminded by workers of "Our Dumb Friends League".

At a recent air raid in March, 18 animals were rescued and included rabbits, cats, birds and a dog. They were taken and cared for at the League's shelter and treated there for shock. Since the raids, members have returned to the scene each day searching for any other pets that needed to be rescued.'

March 29th, 1943

At about 11.10am on Monday 29th March, 1943, four Focke Wulf 190s came across the town, using their canons and machine guns before dropping their 500kg bombs. These were part of a much larger force that had just attacked Brighton where the clinic in Sussex Street (now Morley Street) had been severely damaged and a number of people killed.

These aircraft were members of 10/JG54 and based in Northern France. They were flying at a low altitude, from east to west in two's, line abreast. One pair of these aircraft flew almost the whole length of New Church Road with guns blazing.

One of the first to be killed was Mrs. Lila Langley, a member of the Hove Fire Guard. She was 48 years old and lived at no. 224, New Church Road. She was in her bed recovering from a minor illness. A bullet pierced the window of her bedroom and penetrated her heart, killing her instantly. Her husband had been at work at the time of the incident, and he identified his wife at the hospital.

Having terrorised the townsfolk with their display of machine and cannon fire the attackers released their bombs on various parts of the town. They hit many areas of terraced streets, consisting of houses and small shops.

It was probably the first bomb that scored a direct hit on the Shirley Press, a small printing works in Shirley Street, causing major damage. There were 17 workers in the building at the time and by some miracle none were killed. Three of the employees were struck by molten lead, and two of them had scalp wounds where the lead had settled and then cooled off, clinging to their hair. They were shouting for help, more frightened than severely injured. Others were pinned by the heavy machinery.

Local residents and passers-by arrived just before the main contingent of rescue workers arrived, helping several people from the ruins. The owner of the printing works had a very lucky escape, as he had been called out by a customer just before the raid. His office was completely crushed and he would probably have been killed.

Below: The printing works in Shirley Street suffered a direct hit. (Author's collection)

Right: Another view of Shirley Street after the bombing. Note the military personnel helping with the rescue. (Author's collection)

Meanwhile another very sad tale was unfolding – the sad death of a baby which is told in a later chapter. Mrs Violet Stevens had left her pram outside the local butcher's shop when enemy aircraft machine-gunned the street.

The son of Alderman Thompson JP was among the injured. He was managing his father's shop, which was totally wrecked. When the bomb fell he ducked underneath the counter, and this prompt action probably saved his life as the counter was hit by some large pieces of debris. As it was, some of it struck him on the head and he was covered with blood. He was eventually rescued from the debris with serious head injuries and taken to Hove hospital. His wife, who was at the back of the shop, escaped serious injury. She was treated at the scene and later visited her husband at the hospital.

One of the houses was severely damaged and a woman was trapped beneath the debris. A doctor was called and then lowered into the wreckage. He administered an anaesthetic to her, and as he finished the injection there was a further collapse of the building and the two of them were buried and overcome by coal gas, which was escaping from a broken gas pipe. Two other doctors went to their aid, and ultimately the woman and doctor were rescued from the wreckage to loud cheers from the spectators.

This was the second time that Shirley Street had been bombed. On the first occasion, on 9th April, 1941, residents had woken up to find an unexploded bomb in their street. The street was cordoned off and the bomb was later made safe.

Another bomb hit houses in Nizells Avenue, scoring a direct hit on nos. 5 and 6, killing and injuring several people. Neighbours, as often was the case, were quickly on hand, pulling away the debris with their bare hands. Ambulances and rescuers sped to the scene, arriving within a few minutes. It was obvious that this would entail more help, and soon soldiers from the Canadian regiments joined in. Several middle-aged and elderly people were pulled from the debris. One of the first was George Brotheridge: he was rushed to hospital at Hove but died the following day.

An unusual tale surrounds another victim of this air raid. Alfred Bartlett, from no. 3, Shirley Street, had left his house early that morning to work in the Nizells Avenue area. When the sirens sounded

Sidney Crespin Thompson, the mayor of Brighton from 1930 to 1931, whose wife Ellen was killed when the bomb fell on Nizell's Avenue.

he sought shelter at no. 6, and his luck was certainly out – the bomb hit the house and killed him. Meanwhile, one of the other bombs exploded near his home, causing blast damage to the roof and windows.

Florence Smart, aged 57 years of 24 Windlesham Gardens, Brighton, had left her home to visit her younger sister, Mabel Aickman, at no. 5, Nizells Avenue. They were enjoying a chat together over a cup of tea when the bomb fell. They were both buried under the mountain of rubble, and their bodies were not recovered for almost two days.

Another casualty was 29-year-old Dorothy Akehurst at no. 6. She was pulled from the debris seriously injured and rushed to hospital, but was found to be dead on arrival. Her husband Ronald, a civil defence worker, suffered serious injuries. He stayed at Southlands hospital for a few days and was then transferred to the King Edward VII Sanatorium at Easebourne, near Midhurst. He died there of his injuries on 5th May.

A further victim of the bombing of Nizell's Avenue was Ellen Thompson. She was 61 years old and the wife of a former mayor of Brighton, Sydney Thompson.

Later that day, the German News Agency, flushed with success, stated: 'Fast German fighter-bombers carried out a low level attack on Brighton at noon today. Direct hits were scored on large blocks of houses and traffic establishments.

'On their return flight our pilots attacked military targets in localities of the defence zone at the southern coast with machine guns. A British fighter plane of the Typhoon type was shot down after a short air duel by one of our Focke-Wulf pilots.'

On 30th March, the *Sussex Daily News* published a list of some of those people who were seriously injured in this raid and taken to Hove hospital. They included Sidney Smith, Miss K. Bishop, William Russell, Mrs. Boughton, Thomas Morley, Miss Marsh, Frederick Gardner, Miss Stella Woodward and Miss Caddy.

A funeral notice in the paper read: 'The funeral of Ellen Thompson will take place at the Downs Crematorium at 12 noon on the 1st April. No flowers by request.'

Bomb damage in Nizell's Avenue. (Brighton History Centre)

Above: Bomb damage somewhere in Hove, 1943.

*Below: An ARP enrolment office in a former ladies'
hairdresser's in the New Church Road/Portland Road
area. (Brighton History Centre)*

Peter Gear's Story

Here's another story relating to the raid of Monday 29th March, 1943. Peter Gear wrote it almost 60 years after the event, but it remains as vivid now as it was then. There are some things that happen to you as a child which are never forgotten, as this story proves.

"It began like any other day. I had breakfast and got ready for school. It was the start of a new week at school. I was 10 years old and lived in Shirley Street, Hove, next door to a greengrocer's shop – Blaber's. My house, no. 73, was on the north side of the street and about 150 yards from the junction with Goldstone Street. I lived there with my mother. The street comprised terraced houses stretching along towards Sackville Road. There were several small shops, mainly on the ends of the street at the junctions with Goldstone Street and Sackville Road.

Peter Gear today.

The main building on the junction of Goldstone Street and Shirley Street was the Shirley Press. This was a fairly large printing works, employing a number of people. On the opposite corner was Thompson's hardware shop, with several other small shops nearby. These consisted of a butcher's, a fish and chip shop, a hairdresser's, a dairy and a public house called The Exchange.

I attended Ellen Street junior mixed school, which was just a short walk away from my home. The headmaster was a Mr. Smith and my class teacher was Miss Abbott. As I recall, the day was rather dull and overcast but dry.

It was soon after 11am and the lessons were progressing as normal when suddenly there came the very loud roar of aircraft engines and the violent chattering of machine gun fire. This was so loud that it had to come from immediately outside the school. Miss Abbott shouted out 'under' and we all dived under our respective desks just as we had practised many times. We had hardly got under our desks when the whole school shook, and at the same time there was an almighty thump. We knew a bomb had fallen somewhere nearby. We stayed under the desks, and then after a few minutes the sounds died away and it was quiet. We were told to quickly file out of the classroom and make our way downstairs to the underground air raid shelters. The other classes followed suit. We stayed in the shelters until the 'all clear' was sounded a short time later.

The school suffered no damage, probably because it was too far away from the bomb blast.

At lunchtime I made my way home via my usual route, down Goldstone Street, but the way was blocked at the junction with Livingstone Street by tapes across the road. I saw debris and rubble everywhere around the junction with Shirley Street. I saw that the Exchange Public house and some of the small shops had been badly damaged. However, the worst damage had been inflicted on the Shirley Press, which was a heap of bricks and concrete beams with just a couple of walls still standing. The hardware shop opposite the Press was also badly damaged, and Bert Thompson had been injured when the counter had been blown over onto him.

I had a good look at all the damage, but then thought I had better get home. I entered Shirley Street from the Sackville Road end, and on reaching my house saw smashed windows and slates missing from the roof. Most of the houses in the street were in the same condition, their slates strewn across the roadway. I had a front door key as my mother was out – she did domestic work at a house in King's Gardens on Hove seafront.

I opened the door and went in. The first thing I noticed was the dust and grime over all the furniture: it was a mess. I looked around and saw that eight of our windows had been smashed. I went out into the garden and found that it was littered with bricks and pieces of timber which had been thrown over the gardens from the Shirley Press. The worst damage had been caused by a large lump of concrete that had landed on the roof of our outside toilet, severely damaging it. Anyone in there at the time would have had an almighty headache.

I had to use the toilet next door at no. 75. I think it was about five weeks before ours was repaired.

The only fatality in the incident was a member of the armed forces, home on leave, who was leaving one of the shops (possibly the butcher's) as the bomb exploded.

During the next few days, life returned to some form of normality and to us kids it was all a great big adventure. The next few weeks saw us being chased by the police and the ARP Wardens, as we would burrow into the ruins of the Shirley Press, collecting the lead print to make up sets of the alphabet.

The final thrill of this incident came when, standing with my mates, I watched the old corporation steamroller with a large hawser attached pulling down the remaining walls of the badly damaged properties. As kids we didn't fully understand that we were watching the final destruction of people's homes and livelihoods."

CL 756793

CERTIFIED COPY of an ENTRY OF BIRTH
Pursuant to the Births and Deaths Registration Act 1953

Registration District Brighton

1942. Birth in the Sub-district of Brighton Outer   in the County Borough of Brighton

No.	When and where born	Name, if any	Sex	Name and surname of father	Name, surname and maiden surname of mother	Occupation of father	Signature, description and residence of informant	When registered	Signature of registrar	Name entered after registration
121	Eighth December 1942 Sussex Maternity Hospital U.D.	Peter James Victor	Boy	Horace James Stevens	Violet Stevens formerly Cosham	Electrical Engineer of 44, Byron Street Hove U.D.	H.J. Stevens Father 44, Byron Street Hove	Tenth December 1942	H.E.T. Eggar Registrar	/

Certified to be a true copy of an entry in a register in my custody.

R.J. Ballagher   Deputy Superintendent Registrar

5·5·2000 Date

CAUTION: THERE ARE OFFENCES RELATING TO FALSIFYING OR ALTERING A CERTIFICATE AND USING OR POSSESSING A FALSE CERTIFICATE. ©CROWN COPYRIGHT
WARNING: A CERTIFICATE IS NOT EVIDENCE OF IDENTITY.

HC 694504

CERTIFIED COPY of an ENTRY OF DEATH
Pursuant to the Births and Deaths Registration Act 1953

Registration District Hove

1943. Death in the Sub-district of Hove   in the County of East Sussex

No.	When and where died	Name and surname	Sex	Age	Occupation	Cause of death	Signature, description, and residence of informant	When registered	Signature of registrar
436	Twentyninth March 1943 Hove Hospital Sackville Road Hove U.D.	Peter James Victor Stevens	Male	3 months	of 44. Byron Street Hove. U.D. Son of Horace James Stevens an Electrical Engineer	Due to War Operations	H.J. Stevens Father 44, Byron Street Hove	Thirtieth March 1943	E. Brassington Registrar

Certified to be a true copy of an entry in a register in my custody.

R.J. Ballagher   Deputy Superintendent Registrar

5·5·2000 Date

CAUTION: THERE ARE OFFENCES RELATING TO FALSIFYING OR ALTERING A CERTIFICATE AND USING OR POSSESSING A FALSE CERTIFICATE. ©CROWN COPYRIGHT
WARNING: A CERTIFICATE IS NOT EVIDENCE OF IDENTITY.

The Death of a Baby

This is the saddest of stories from the war years, about probably the youngest victim of enemy action in our area. I am obliged to Peter Jackson, Grace Scutt, William Willard, and Colin Wilsher for their help with the details of it.

Peter Stevens was born at the Sussex Maternity Hospital, Brighton, on Tuesday 8th December 1942, his birth (facing page, top) being registered two days later. His parents were Horace and Violet Stevens, who lived at 44, Byron Street in Hove. He was 40, she was 39, and, married for all of 16 years, they were desperate for a child. Not surprisingly, therefore, they were absolutely delighted with their baby, doting on his every movement. Violet used to take Peter out in his large pram, proudly showing him off at every opportunity.

As the weeks passed, Peter grew steadily, putting on the correct weight – a beautiful, 'bonny' baby much loved by the neighbours. They would stop Mrs Stevens in order to get a good look at him.

On Monday 29th March, 1943, he was just 16 weeks old. He was in his pram as his mother pushed him along Byron Street on her way to the local shops. She stopped to talk to neighbours and it was just after 11am that she arrived at George Smith's butcher's shop at no 51, Shirley Street.

She carefully put the brake on, securing the pram, and went inside. Seconds later the sirens sounded and German Focke-Wulf 190s from 10 Staffel Jagdgeschwader 54 appeared overhead. As the bombs fell the German aircraft opened up with their guns and deliberately raked the streets of Hove.

The butcher attempted to restrain Violet, but she rushed out of the shop to collect her little son. It was too late: whether intentionally or not, some of the bullets had struck Peter's pram. She picked him up, calling out that her baby was hurt, and ran along the streets to Hove General Hospital. Half crying and half screaming, she was desperate for medical help.

When she arrived at the hospital she was gently told that there was nothing that could be done. Peter was pronounced dead on arrival. Violet was treated for severe shock – a shock that she would never get over but would have to learn to live with.

The baby's death was registered by his father the following day, the certificate (page 106, bottom) stating that death was 'Due to war operations' – such cold words.

On Thursday 1st April, parents, relatives and friends attended the funeral at Hove Cemetery. The street was lined with neighbours all crying and hugging each other in their grief. Peter was buried at grave no. 534, block 3.

Family and neighbours offered his parents every support, but although they always put on a brave face, behind closed doors they were very sad people. Their worst day afterwards was the first anniversary of the incident that robbed Peter of his young life, but the grief never went away: desperate though they had been for a child, Peter's death in such tragic circumstances would mean that they were unable to face having another baby. They eventually died childless, still living at the same address in Byron Street.

Violet died in 1970, two days before her 67th birthday, while Horace lived on until 1982, dying at the age of 80.

25th May, 1943

At about 12.30pm on Tuesday 25th May 1943 four Focke-Wulf 190s – part of the group that had just been involved in a bombing attack on Brighton – screamed across the Hove skies with machine guns and canons blazing, raking the streets of the town. They followed the line of New Church Road westwards and lined up the gasholders. They scored many direct hits with their fire, and set the gasholders on fire, the flames reaching more than 50ft high. The attack was over almost as soon as it began, the German aircraft disappearing across the sea to their bases.

The fire service was soon on the scene and valiantly fought the huge fire caused by the gas. They would be so engaged for close on five hours before they brought the blaze under control. As a result of this attack the residents would be without their gas supply for a couple of days. Minor repairs were undertaken to restore a minimum

Beach repairs in Hove shortly before the end of the war. (Brighton History Centre)

supply, but in the end it would be some months before the full capacity of the gas works could be restored.

The repairs to the gasworks would be subject of several letters and discussions by the local town council who were very annoyed by the length of time it took to regain full capacity.

A report dated 26th June stated that the gasholder was still under repair, and that a date of completion could not be estimated. A further report, dated 11th September, stated that repairs were still being carried out but were not yet completed. On the 22nd November a further report found that repairs were still being carried out, and another of 16th December said much the same.

The gasholder repairs were finally completed on 12th May 1944, a long and lengthy job.

May 28th, 1944

Saturday 28th May 1944 was but ten minutes old when the final air attack on the town occurred. This was quite late in the war and a little more than a week before the Allied landings in Normandy. The town was full of Allied soldiers and other servicemen as well as their military equipment.

The town was fast asleep as the sirens wailed the impending danger a few minutes after midnight. Many of the residents decided not to take to the shelters – after all, there been no air attacks for more than a year and this was surely a false alarm. On this occasion they were wrong, as an enemy aircraft came in from the southeast and dropped two high explosive bombs as it crossed over the town.

The first fell in York Avenue, exploding on a house where servicemen were billeted. This resulted in the deaths of three soldiers and serious injuries to another 11. Seven others were

Bomb crater in York Avenue after the May raid. (Brighton History Centre)

treated for minor injuries. Serious damage was caused to the house and to those adjoining it. Blast damage was caused to around 30 homes in the immediate vicinity, while some 120 houses suffered roof and window damage over a wider area.

Rescue workers were soon on the scene, while the service colleagues of the injured carried out first aid. A fleet of ambulances ferried those most seriously injured to Hove Hospital, and another three were taken to the Royal Sussex County Hospital. The bodies of two of the servicemen were not located until about mid-afternoon, and the large pile of rubble and debris was still being removed more than 36 hours later.

The second bomb fell on open ground at Toads Hole Farm. There were no casualties, but two small farm buildings were slightly damaged and a large crater was created.

York Avenue: another view of the crater. (Brighton History Centre)

Beachcombing in a Minefield

An inquest was held at Southwick on Friday 1st September 1944 on two men who were killed by a beach mine. Alfred Sherrard of no. 7, Viaduct Road in Brighton and Ronald Edward Hoyles of Tamworth Road in Hove had both worked as fitters' mates, and they had gone beachcombing in their dinner hour.

William Owers, one of their colleagues, said that he was at work when he heard an explosion on the beach shortly before 1pm. He knew that the two men had been in the habit of going there. He went along the road at the top of the beach and met a man called Tyson, who told him that two men had just been killed and that another had been seriously wounded. A policeman was trying to get through the barbed wire to get to the injured man.

Mr. Owers said that he went along to see if he could be of any help. He saw the injured man – a fellow workmate named George Hibling who lived at St.Nicholas' Road, Brighton – sitting on the beach, by the side of a crater and attended by a policeman. The bodies of the two men were on the beach about 20 yards away.

A War Department notice warns of danger on the beaches.

Dr. James Latigan, giving medical evidence, said that both men had suffered multiple injuries. Their bodies were badly mutilated and death would have been instantaneous.

Lawrence Tyson, another workman, said that he saw two men go on to the beach. He heard an explosion and saw a cloud of smoke about 400 or 500 yards away. He was asked to fetch an ambulance and was told that two men had been killed and another blinded.

Captain Charles Cant said that in his opinion the minefield was adequately protected. There was a barbed wire fence, 4ft high, with warning notices – in fact there was a warning notice about three yards from the crater.

Sergeant Hawthornwaite said a passage had been forced through the barbed wire of the minefield. The minefield was completely barricaded by a barbed wire fence. The only possible way of getting onto it was through a gap which had been made to enable workmen to go down and perform essential work. The sergeant added that around the minefield there was no gap. There were War Department warning notices at regular intervals of 40 yards on the north side of the barricade, although these notices could only be read by people walking along the road. There was a very large notice by the gap stating that the area was prohibited and access not allowed.

The district coroner, F.W. Butler, recorded a verdict of accidental death, saying that it appeared that all necessary precautions to prevent such an occurrence had been taken. Although the fencing was efficient and warning notices were displayed, the men had taken their lives in their own hands.

At the conclusion of the inquest a brigadier said that he had prepared a statement on behalf of the military authorities which he would like to read, and a copy of which he would like to hand to the press.

He began to read it out, but the solicitor acting for the widow of one of the men intervened, expressing a very strong objection to it. He described the statement as a 'verbal castigation of the dead men', and it was withdrawn before it had been fully read.

Doreen Hyde's Wartime Memories

"I was 12 years old in 1939 when the Second World War started and was living in York Avenue, Hove. I was attending the Westcombe School in Dyke Road Avenue at this time. I remember the start of the war to be one of excitement tinged with fear. I suppose the fear was the thought of the unknown.

In York Avenue the Army took over an empty house and their lorries were parked all up the road under the trees. On Wednesday evenings an army band played in St. Anne's Well Gardens. It was lovely and enjoyed by everyone who attended or lived in the vicinity. Air raid shelters were dug in these gardens close by Nizell's Avenue. While the shelters were being dug they unearthed a coal-like substance. This caused quite a lot of interest, but it didn't burn and so the interest quickly faded.

My school days at Westcombe continued as usual except for having to carry a gas mask as well as my schoolbooks whenever I went to my lessons. During the air raids we went to the school shelter and if the sirens sounded at going home time then we stayed at school until the 'All clear' siren went. Although we often spent time during the nights in our home shelters and had interrupted sleep, we were still expected to do our homework and to do it on time and arrive at school on time.

In 1943, when I was 16 years old I was a member of the Girl Guides, and I think it was at this age that you had to register with the authorities. In the Guides we were involved with all sorts of interesting duties. One day a week during the school holidays I went to the Civic restaurant in London Road to work. This place had been an empty shop, and after some work had been done it was turned into a quite smart restaurant. Here you could have a lunch for 6d. My job was usually to serve pink sauce over a white steamed pudding. At the end of this little job I was offered a free meal, but I declined – I had seen rather too much pink sauce.

The Westcombe School (Hove) Guide Company decided to open a 'salvage shop' during the Easter Holidays of 1943. A friend and I visited local house estate agents asking them to lend us an empty shop for the purpose we intended. (We traded on our fathers' good names: they were business people which possibly led them to think that we were a couple of sensible people.) Finally, an estate agent in Preston Street, Brighton allowed us to use an empty greengrocer's shop nearby.

We got the shop cleaned up and ready with some help and it duly opened, having used one of my father's builder's trucks to transport the goods. We collected a large variety of things, such as waste paper, bottles, jam jars, electric light bulbs, cotton reels, old batteries from torches, tins, saucepans, cardboard and tinfoil. These were all placed in vegetable holders.

We had one problem and that was the shutter on the outside of the shop – it was far too heavy for us to put up and down. The problem was soon solved, as the local beat policeman did it for us. I often wondered if he was around just to keep an eye on us.

We very soon became well known for this act of 'national service', and we had our picture in the *Sussex Daily News*, complete with a good write-up. On one occasion the mayor paid us a visit. I then

The Girl Guides worked hard during the war. Doreen Hyde stands second from the left outside their 'salvage shop'. (Doreen Hyde)

went a step further and with the family collected apples, plums and blackberries preserved in salt, pickled eggs and even stinging nettles, which were cooked and eaten like spinach. We really enjoyed these times – they were such good fun.

One day (29th March 1943) a number of bombs were dropped very close to our house. We thought that they had been aimed at the laundry on the corner of Nizell's Avenue, which was the Wick Laundry. One bomb fell in York Avenue, causing damage in the road and a number of houses suffered blast damage. Bombs also fell in Addison Road, Colbourne Road and Nizell's Avenue. It was an awful mess and a number of people were killed.

Thinking back, the time I felt most scared was when I saw parts of the two piers removed. I thought that the invasion by the Germans must be very close.

The fear, I suppose, was slightly tempered by the fact that every Friday evening our home was 'open house' for anyone who wished to join us to play darts in our kitchen, warmed in winter by the boiler. However much of the war was a worrying time, there was a wonderful feeling of fellowship and trust amongst the people as we shared what we had – including our homes – with friends, with neighbours and, at times, with strangers."

Above: Salute the Soldier Week, April 1944. The mayor takes the salute at Hove Town Hall. (Brighton History Centre)

Below: Victory in Europe parade in May, 1945, as seen from the King Alfred in Kingsway, Hove. (Brighton History Centre)

The War Ends

It was now January 1945. Was this the year that the war would at last come to an end, the year that everyone had prayed for? The bombing was certainly over, and for the younger people of the country entertainment began to figure more prominently in their lives once more.

The cinema, theatre and dancing were always at the top of the list, and now they could be enjoyed without the threat of air raids. People were becoming more relaxed. Food rationing continued, but many people were sure they could see the end of that in sight: just how wrong were they to be!

At the beginning of the year the pantomime at the Grand Theatre was *Where the Rainbow Ends*, and it enjoyed full audiences for most of the shows.

As the months passed by, thousands of aircraft filled the skies over southern England on their way across the Channel, carrying bombs to drop on the enemy forces. People were expecting the end of the war by springtime.

The news about the war in Europe seemed to get better and better each day. By the 19th January almost all of Poland had been liberated. By the end of the month Russian troops were just 70 miles from Berlin.

At home there was also good news of a lighter nature. Brighton and Hove Albion beat Arsenal 3–0 in a really good game and soon afterwards defeated Brentford 5–3 in a cup match. This was followed by a 6–2 victory over Millwall, who had the great Tommy Lawton playing for them.

The barbed wire defences along the sea front were being dismantled after almost six years, which in itself was a tonic for residents. By the end of February the whole of the seafront road along to Roedean was fully open, as was the Undercliff Walk, while people could bathe in the sea at Black Rock again. Good Friday, 30th March, saw the re-opening of the beach area from the Grand Hotel along to the borough boundary.

People at this stage were beginning to dismantle their Morrison

Drumhead service at Sussex County Cricket Ground, Hove, May 19th, 1945. (Brighton History Centre)

shelters, while their Anderson shelters became handy storage spaces.

On 27th April Russian and American forces linked up: the final stages of the war were being played out. Lloyd's Bank in Kemp Town certainly thought that the war was almost at an end, as they took great pains to put out their flagpole ready for the great day.

The day everyone had been waiting for fell on 8th May – Victory in Europe (V.E.) Day. This was an occasion for great celebrations. Winston Churchill made the historic speech at 3pm. Locally, thousands of people flocked into the streets, dancing and making the town reminiscent of a giant dance hall. The town came to a standstill. The Academy and the Odeon in West Street and the Regent at the Clock Tower were all lit up. Flags were hung from windows in hundreds of houses and shops. The mayors of Brighton and Hove read the proclamation from their town halls.

People were reminded that the war in the Far East continued and that the war wasn't quite finished yet, but this dampened spirits not a bit. Street parties were organised throughout the town – mainly for the children, although it was the adults who possibly had the most fun.

On 13th May there was a large victory parade through the town, the salute being taken by Brighton's mayor in the Pavilion grounds. The newspapers carried the story that 'Lord Haw Haw' (William Joyce) had been captured, and soon afterwards that his life had terminated at the end of a rope.

There suddenly seemed to be more cars on the road as the basic petrol ration was returned. Winston Churchill resigned and the wartime coalition government came to an end. At the first elections, on 5th July, Clement Attlee became the prime minister and Churchill led the opposition.

The whole of the beaches were now deemed to be safe and were finally opened to the public in July. They were packed, as a heatwave covered the whole of the county. Before the month was over the lights along the seafront were switched on for the first time since 1939: the mass of twinkling lights made a wonderful sight. Now, the people finally knew that the blackouts were well and truly behind them. It was a time to celebrate and a time to live.

Many workers in the town were granted two days off to celebrate the end of the war, declared on 15th August 1945 after the surrender of Japan. A great day – no more fighting.

As usual the centre of the celebrations in Brighton was the Clock Tower, and the crowds grew and grew as the day unfolded. At the bottom of West Street a group of soldiers led the singing of patriotic songs, each verse getting louder and louder as the crowds grew attracted by the singing, dancing and shouting.

On the waste ground near the top of West Street someone lit a bonfire, using the rubbish that had gathered there, but the police thought it a little dangerous and it was quickly extinguished. People were using whistles to create as much noise as possible, and then fireworks began to go off: it was deafening, and it at first startled many people for whom it was all too reminiscent of the bombs and the machine-gunning they had had to endure. The fun went on all night.

On the 23rd October came a massive gale which lasted for a full four days and caused a great deal of damage.

On November 5th the town enjoyed its first bonfire celebrations for more than five years, the government having lifted the ban on fireworks.

But as this momentous year came to an end, it also brought some sad news. On 21st December it was announced that General 'Blood and Guts' Patton, the famous military general, had died as a result of a motoring accident.

And then came Christmas, the first peacetime celebration for so many years. To return to the feasting of earlier times would, of course, take several years, but although food was still rationed, every effort was to create something special, and most families achieved something with at least an echo of those happier days before the war.

Crowds outside Brighton town hall in Bartholomews Square listen to the declaration of the end of the war in Europe in May, 1945. (Brighton History Centre)

Acknowledgements

It is rare to write a book without the help of other people, and I wish to record my thanks to the following, who assisted me in the production of this one.

I often request stories from members of the public and, as in this case, I usually receive a very good response: my thanks to all those who took time to write out their wartime stories and help me in my own personal research.

A special mention to Bob Elliston, who gave me both photographs and information, to East Sussex Record Office who supplied me with various documents, and to Brighton History Centre who made available to me a large number of their wartime photographs.

I am grateful to David Arscott, whose editorial skills always make my books look much better than they otherwise would.

And, lastly, thanks to my wife, Christine. I still don't quite understand how I get away with causing our place to become so untidy after she has devoted time to making it look so nice. I do finally tidy up, but in quite a lame fashion.

A group of wardens from 12D group in Brighton in October, 1944. Note the white hats in front of them. (Brighton History Centre)

The Brighton Zylo Works, also pictured on page 2, was involved throughout the war in making aircraft instruments for navigation. (David Maltby, Zylo Works)